# Called
## to the
# Mountains

The Story of Jean L. Frese

*To Kathy,*
*Blessings to you!*

as told to

GRETCHEN GRIFFITH

*Gretchen Griffith*

*Called to the Mountains*
The story of Jean L. Frese
As told to Gretchen Griffith

Printed in the United States of America

Unless otherwise noted, all Scripture quotations are taken from the King James Version of the Bible.

Library of Congress Control Number: 2013910369

Cover Photo: Bonita Swanger
Insert Photograph: Troupe's Studio
Front Photo Design: Andrew Pitts Photography
Back Cover Art: Bonita Swanger
Cover Design: Brian Thigpen

ISBN-13: 978-1489526670
ISBN-10: 1489526676

# DEDICATED

To the memory of

Major Cecil Brown

Founder of the Mountain Mission

# ACKNOWLEDGMENTS

Inspiration for this memoir came from Mrs. Lt. Col. Patsy Tritton.

Previously published stories told by Major Jean Frese in Major Frank Duracher's *Smoky Mountain High, the Consuming Passion of Cecil Brown*, Crest Books, 2007 are included with permission granted from the Salvation Army National Publications.

Special appreciation to Bonita Swanger, Clyde, North Carolina; Ray Rouser Photography, Waynesville, North Carolina; Harry Joiner, Troup's Studio, Toccoa, Georgia; Glinka Studio formerly of Donora, Pennsylvania; The Historical Society, Donora, Pennsylvania; Andrew Pitts Photography, Lenoir, North Carolina; The Book Maker, Lenoir, North Carolina; and to the many friends of Jean Frese who donated personal photographs through the years.

# PREFACE

A road winding deep into the North Carolina Smoky Mountains takes the harried traveler from the busyness of a highway into the peacefulness of a retreat. "Fine's Creek," the sign announces. Off Interstate-40, this is one of the last exits before the Tennessee state line. A turn to the right, another turn, this to the left, and a narrow road leads up the side of a mountain. Bare, leafless trees hugging the cliffs allow glimpses of truck caravans snaking the interstate alongside the Pigeon River gorge below. The road twists up, high, even higher to another turn to the left into a compound labeled Shelton Laurel Mission of the Salvation Army. It ends at a small, unassuming house, although the brave soul with a four wheel drive vehicle could continue on, down, down then up again, to the mission's graveyard.

In that graveyard sits a tombstone awaiting the day its future occupant will be called to glory. Etched beneath the name and birth date and empty space reserved for the date of death is one simple sentence, "Thank you God for bringing me to the mountains."

Its owner greets this traveler in her nearby house, eager to tell the story of why she is thankful to her Lord for doing exactly that, calling her to a life of service in the mountains. They are kin, cousins from two generations, their relationship more likened to that of aunt and niece, Jean the teller, Gretchen the storycatcher author, the daughter of Jean's cousin, Frances.

No ordinary home, this one's shrunken proportions match the almost doll-like frame of the retired Salvation Army Major the traveler has come to interview. Here, in the shelter of pine and laurel and rhododendron, Jean Frese, also known as Lorraine, has found her most comfortable piece of the world and seeks to set for the record what God has done in her life.

Her car is backed into its usual spot at the entrance. Her dog announces an arrival well ahead of any footsteps. Jean ignores the constant barking that fluctuates from gentle yips to frenzied yelps. Shushing the Pomeranian, Cheenie, she apologizes over the messy room. Her hair, gray for more years than not, is gathered into a bun. Two hints that she is nearing ninety years of age, the walker and the cane, sit to the side, just in case. On this day, she uses neither.

Beyond the kitchen, in a section clearly designed to keep the dog out, is the sitting area. Unlike the room at the main entrance, this is more formal, a preacher parlor. Not a separate room at all, this back corner is partitioned off from the kitchen by a knee high, practically waist high to Jean, wooden barrier reminiscent of an altar rail extending from one side of the room to the other. A solid gate in its middle swings shut quickly, preventing Cheenie from entering, and protecting the stuffed furniture, throw blankets and hand crafted quilts from wear and tear and incessant shedding.

Although the lamps above the settee, one to the left, one to the right, offer little illumination, the several ever-present, ever-lit ceramic Christmas trees cheerfully add a warm glow. There, amidst the many ceramic deer, sheep and tiny glistening trees, surrounded by photographs, relics and antiques of her past, Major Jean Frese, also known as Lorraine, recounts her life. Her voice is full of mountain culture, wizened through years of experience, often wandering in her simple way of explaining her mission, her calling. The author presses record and the story, much of it hidden away and forgotten through the years, gushes out like a pure Smoky Mountain spring finding its way to the surface. In her own words, Jean Lorraine Frese witnesses of being "Called to the Mountains."

# 1

*I will lift up mine eyes unto the hills,*

*from whence cometh my help.* **Psalm 121:1**

God's been good to me. He knew when I needed help and he gave it to me. He knew I couldn't do it myself, so He always provided me with somebody at the right time. The Lord did one more thing for me. He called me to the mountains. I've said many times, "Thank you, Lord, for calling me to the mountains."

I started out life surrounded by mountains, the Alleghenies, but I was not surrounded by family like most people are. I was born in Pittsburgh, Pennsylvania in 1926 and named after a relative of my mother's, Province Lorraine Reed, my grandmother's sister. I never did have a middle name, though. Back then, I was only Lorraine.

I did not know much about my family, not even that my mother's name was Mary until I went up to the graveyard and saw it on her tombstone. People always called her Jean. She was divorced and although she was very sick, she still had to work. She couldn't take care of us, my sister Ruth and me. Ruth was older and went to live with our Aunt Glad, Gladys Laughlin. After Ruth grew up, she joined the Navy as a nurse stationed in the Philippines and later the Solomon Island, and then married, had two children and lived in Seattle, Washington. My sister Ruth didn't have a middle name either, so she picked herself one, called herself Betty, Betty Ruth.

3

My life turned out completely different from my sister's. I was sent to a boarding home until I was five years old. My mother paid to have me put in there. It was like an orphanage, a boarding house for children from first born, up to when they were five years old. Only the children lived there and hired people would come and go, whoever was supposed to be on duty that particular shift. My mother worked in the hospital as a maid, so it must have been close by there. I hardly remember anything about living in the home, not even its name. One year at Halloween the workers wanted to entertain the little children and some of them came running down the stairs with a false face on. Instead we all got scared and ran outside. That I do remember.

When I turned five years old I was supposed to have moved out, but they couldn't let me go at that time because I

Six years old.
(Glinka Studio)

was too sick. I had German measles so bad I had to stay at the home until I got well. First they sent me to my grandmother's house in Donora, Pennsylvania, then to my Uncle John's house out in the country, still in the mountains, not all that far from Pittsburgh. His wife wanted me to live with them because she had lost a child, but she was very sickly and the family didn't think that she could handle me. One day they took me over to Fellsburg to my Aunt Etha, my mother's sister, for her to make clothes for me to start school. I never returned to Uncle John's.

Aunt Etha said, "The door is open for anyone who wants to come in the family. Just walk in." She accepted me. A lot of places, when you go as an outsider, they show partiality, but my aunt never did. She was as good to me as she was to her own children. Finally I was surrounded by family. And mountains.

My first day I went there, I remember well. Aunt Etha and Uncle Thomas and three of their children were there, Glad (named for my Aunt Gladys who had taken in my sister), and the boys Elmer and Jim. Two other children, Frances and Marion, were grown and had moved out. That very day my aunt and uncle were taking out the wood stove and putting in an electric stove. I had on long handle underwear, as always. I wore them all the time at the boarding house because they wouldn't let me take them off. That day was too hot, time for summer clothes, so Glad wanted them off. "Get them long handles off her."

My aunt said, "You can't just do that. We'll have to gradually take them off." I had to adjust to so many different things, even the underwear.

Uncle Thomas had three huge fields, about three acres each and that's what they lived on. My aunt had bad heart trouble, couldn't help with the farming. Her legs would swell and water would come out of the pores and she would ask me to bathe them.

The boys Elmer and Jim would tease me, especially Jim. When I was about ten, he got a stool and put me up on it. I was scared of heights so I started screaming murder. Aunt Etha, I called her Mom by then, came a-running, shouting, "What are you boys doing to her?" Before she got there they grabbed me and put me down on the floor.

"Nothing. She just started to holler."

That's boys.

One time the boys went upstairs, went to bed. Their room was fixed so that the window opened on to a roof and they could climb down onto a tree and get out. That night they went up to the church where there was a big cliff and then a ditch, right in front of the churchyard. They stuffed blue jeans and a shirt and laid it down in the gully and called the police saying that somebody's dead. They ran home and crawled back in the bed. The police suspicioned them. He came to the door, the policeman did, and said "I want to see your boys. They called us on a false alarm."

My aunt would never, never lie, even for her kids. "Well, they're in the bed sleeping." Then the police left and they didn't tell their mother the truth for years. That's boys and they were ornery.

Of course I got into things myself, but not too bad. What I would do were little things, like I would go over to see my girlfriend, a classmate Eliza Naylor. I would go up in the orchard and circle back around and slip over to her house. My aunt happened to see me slip back over one day and she got on me.

I have a picture hanging on my wall today that hung in the hall back then. Underneath it there was a round chair. They would get the fly swatter out and give me a whipping on that chair. I don't have that chair, but I have the memory of the picture above it.

Before I had left the boarding house, this woman had set me down on stool at the counter where we ate and said, "Now I'm going to tell you, when you get some food you like," she says, "hide it. Keep it, so you can go back to it later."

I loved applesauce. When I came to my aunt's I hid it, the applesauce. They were cleaning the living room one day. They don't very often move the piano to get behind it because it was so heavy, but they moved it this day and they found the applesauce where I had hid it. I don't know how long it had been there, but it was long enough for it to mold.

At school, the old Lebanon School, when you were bad you'd get a whipping. When I was in first grade the teacher tried to whip me in the seat. She took the paddle and tried to hit me and I'd bounce from one side of the seat to the other. When I was in sixth grade we had three grades all in one classroom. I was sitting in the back and wanted to talk to somebody in the front, so I crawled there on my hands and knees. Got a spanking.

The children took turns cleaning the schoolhouse back then. I said to one of the kids as we were working, "You know this is a chicken coop, don't you?" It looked just like a chicken coop to me and to prove myself I said, "See that corn?" I didn't tell her, but the town folks in the area would play bingo there at night and they used corn to mark as each number was called out.

I was living with my aunt when my mother was sick in the hospital in Pittsburgh. I was fourteen and my aunt said to me, "Honey, you're an orphan now." My mother had died, had been dead a week and nobody knew about it. Her body was in the freezer until somebody claimed her. I don't think my aunt realized how that hurt me.

My cousin Glad did. She stepped up, went and got me a bicycle to help me through that sad time. When I was riding it, my hands would swell and I got a crazy idea in my head. Earlier the grownups had been talking and I was listening in. They said that grandmother had real bad swelling caused by water gathering up in her hand.

I had it in my mind that I would too and if I just won't drink so much water, my hands wouldn't swell. When I would ride the bicycle, it would be hot. I'd be looking at my hands and I couldn't even close them, they swelled so bad.

I liked to go swimming at the pool in West Newton, six miles away, and I'd ride my bicycle there every chance I got. A lot of the kids from Fellsburg would go there, too. Sometimes Glad would

At my aunt's house with my sister. 1940

drive and she'd take us to a lake to swim, even up to Lake Erie.

My aunt would never let me in the kitchen so I never learned to cook. The only time I was allowed in there was when I was bad and had to wash dishes for punishment. I hate to wash dishes to this day because of that. Because my aunt wasn't well, her other daughter, Frances, would come home from boarding at her teaching job, clean house, straighten up and put things back where she thought they were supposed to be. We couldn't find anything and had to wait until she would come back for her next visit. We'd make a joke about it. "Well, when Fran comes back, we'll find out where it's at."

Glad tried to teach me a little since my aunt did everything for us. She taught me how to clean a sewing machine, how to dust those little tiny grooves in those old timey treadle sewing machines. She tried to train me a little bit for something. She also tried to teach me how to read, but it got the best of her. She'd say "Aaah," and give up on me.

My aunt sat down with me and she's the one who taught me to read. "Now Lorraine, if you don't know a word," she says, "skip over it and you can go back to it and guess and then you'll know what it is." You know, I'm still doing that today. She helped me in a lot of other ways like that. My aunt would read my books to me and then I would go give a report. I scratched and got through school.

My cousin Glad took care of me. She was older than me, already finished college, and stayed with us for a long, long time. The school kind of got it in for her because she had a little more education than the rest of the teachers and then they took it out on me. Glad knew that's why my grades went down because I just gave up. Then one day the lady that was teaching there was onto Glad about something and blessed her out right there in front of the children. I said, "Glad, why didn't you speak up and say something?"

She answers, "Well if I did, I'd be evil like her." I found out later that the reason this teacher got the job was that her husband was on the school board. They left to New York and the police caught them because they were in the mafia.

Then I had a substitute teacher. Oh, was she good. She said "I want you to read this book," and she put it to the level I could read. I read the whole book. First time I ever read a book, sixth grade. Other times, I would look at the funny papers. I would always study the geography book because it was the biggest book I could hide the funny paper in. I never even tried to study until I got out of school, really when I had to study, had to learn things and finally admitted, "Whoa, this has got to stop." I went to Rostraver High School about six miles away. There was a bus, but the last year I rode my bicycle so I could come home sooner.

A neighbor, Thelma Knight Cuthbert, one of the first dear friends the Lord sent to me.
(Glinka Studio)

When my aunt and uncle wanted to be by themselves, they would give me twelve cents to go to the movies and I'd walk to Donora. I lived at the top of a steep hill about three miles away. At the foot of the hill, just before I crossed the Monongahela River bridge, I would pass the little town of Webster. That's where the vegetation was so bad because of the pollution from the steel mills. Actually there was no vegetation at all. When I went back years later I said, "Look! There's vegetation up on that hill." First time I had ever seen it green like that.

They liked to travel and I went with them on a few trips. On a trip south to Florida, we visited the Cherokee Indian Reservation in North Carolina. I never imagined that one day I would end up living nearby.

My aunt and my uncle died early, probably from breathing the

Stopping at a tourist shop in Cherokee.

polluted air. He worked in the steel mill, worked in the coal mines, worked on the road for the WPA, and then he worked the fields, just to make a living. He had the mumps and we tried to get him to stay home. "No I can't. Somebody's going to grab my shovel just as soon as I leave." He died first, then my aunt, although she was ill all the time I lived there. When I graduated high school in 1945, she died that very summer.

I didn't see then, but I can see now how God was protecting me. My aunt died, but the Lord was with me all the time because I got to finish school before it happened. I stayed there at their house that summer. My cousin Glad was trying to get me married off because people thought I'd never make anything of myself. She'd bring this one and then she'd bring that one. She was worried about me and she figured if I got married, that would make it easy, but I wasn't going to get married. I said, "Well, Mother didn't make it and I'm not going to get married." That was my attitude. It was not a Christian attitude. It was just my attitude.

I had finished high school and then I decided to leave. The Lord had his hands on me way back then and sent people who watched over me and took care of me. Glad called up my sister Ruth and she sent me money to go on to school. I took that money and went to Pittsburgh to the Louise Salenger School of Dress Design and Millinery.

I stayed at the Salvation Army facility called the Evangeline Residence located downtown right along the Monongahela River where the boats were. It was for young women who were working or who went on to schooling after high school. They had a different place for unmarried mothers, women in that kind of situation, but this was for business people, single women, a protection for them in the big city. We were sheltered there from the outside world. If you were late coming in, you had to go to the manager's office, to see Captain Huddy Lyons. He wanted you to tell why you were late to make sure you were not doing anything bad. I didn't know much about the Salvation Army except what I would see on the streets at Open Air. I had a curiosity about them and wanted to find out what was going on, but didn't want anybody to see me, so I would hide behind a building and peep out and watch the meetings they were having on the streets. I couldn't understand. They were all wearing the same kind of dark uniforms, looking so funny in those black outfits and the bonnets on. At that point I never imagined that one day I would be one of them.

After I graduated from the millinery school, I went to find a job on my own. I had five dollars and that had to last until I got a job and got paid. I was too shy, wouldn't ask anyone for food or for help. I ate a five cent candy bar for breakfast and supper and a twenty-five cent hamburger at lunch to make it through. I had moved out of the residence

Evangeline Residence in Pittsburgh.
We lived upstairs above the chapel.

and lived with two other girls in the YMCA for fifty cents a night, and we slept on the floor. First I went to a factory where they made caps for eye drops, the rubber part. I didn't stay there very long because a lot of girls made the manager mad. He said to me when one girl left, "Well, she's left me. She got another job. When are you going to leave?" That made me mad so I swallowed my pride and went back to the school to ask for help. They had said they would help find me a job and they found me one as a milliner at Joseph Horne Company, a department store downtown. When I began making a salary I was able to move back into the Evangeline Residence.

I had a little bit of training in school but I said, "I want any job but making hats. I don't care about having any friends, all I have to do is walk the chalk line," and don't you know, I got a job making custom designed hats. One of my clients there was Kathryn Kuhlman, very famous evangelist, faith healer, preached all over the United States. She had services in the big Presbyterian Church in Pittsburgh and I went to a lot of them. She came in the store for me to tack a veil on her hat. Someone asked her, "Don't you get nervous when you get up to preach?" She says, "I'm scared to death but I get in the pulpit and it all goes away." Jimmy Stewart's mother and dad came in, too. They were both tall, built a little bit heavier than him.

Like I say, the Lord had his eye on me from the very beginning. He knew I was petulant, that I wanted to get out. I wanted to do things, explore. I said to some girls working with me, "Take me into this saloon," the one called The Brass Rail. They had spittoons on the floor where a man could spit tobacco into it. I had never seen a place like that. This girl, I knew she drank a lot, said, "The Salvation Army is watching you. I wouldn't dare to take you in there." I knew she was having a lot of trouble and actually the Army was trying to help her. She was trying to walk a chalk line and I was begging her to go here and there, knowing she once went to those kinds of places. She was scared of the Army, it was sort of like a rehab place for her and she had to behave. Even then as an almost grown young woman, I didn't know there was trouble. But she knew it.

I never did get in The Brass Rail. God was protecting me right there.

When I was working at Joseph Horne's I was the youngest one in the group, some of them old enough to be my grandmother. I didn't have all that much money. I would go to the drug store to have lunch and I'd see all these young girls coming in with only one button fastened or using pins to close their blouses. I felt so sorry for them. I asked the waitress, "Who are these girls? What's all these girls doing?" She said they worked at the burlesque show. I thought that if you did that, you got a lot of money, but these girls looked poor.

I went back to work at the millinery department and asked the people I worked with to take me to the burlesque show. The oldest woman there said there was a movie star in that show that she had admired and had gone downhill. She said, "I'll go with you because I want to see what happened." There were five of us that went to that show. I thought that was the worst thing I had ever seen. This man, I think they hired him to go "Aaawwww. EEEE." It was sickening. Striptease. All the motions. It was terrible. We got out of there, the other ladies ahead of me. I walked outside and I couldn't find my friends nowhere. Here they were across the street, way down, where nobody would know they had been there. It was just me alone. I had wanted to see what the other side of the world was like and I saw it. I understood right then that if I didn't have the protection of the Army I could have innocently, with curiosity, gotten in to trouble. I was that adventurous.

When I got to work the next day, would you believe, you know this is where I say the Lord watches out for me, the girls came and got me in the corner. Do you know who spoke to them about it? Our boss. "Ooh, did she get all over us for taking you to that place," those girls said. But it was my idea to go! Even through that the Lord was watching out for me.

Everybody wanted to be my mother when I was in Pittsburgh. I don't know why, I had that innocent look, I guess. There were two in particular, Huddy Lyons and his wife. He was in charge, but evidentially she talked to that girl, the one who I tried to get to take me places like the Brass Rail, told her not to take me to any of those places. A city is very dangerous and I really was innocent when it comes to the outside. I know that I was venturesome and I understand it, because I wanted to know everything. What did happen was God was preparing me a path and I didn't even realize it.

I became active in the Girl Guards, a youth group similar to the Girl Scouts. I had some experience with scouting when my cousin Glad was a leader at home, going along with the Girl Scouts by going with her. Once when we were hiking at a falls, I fell in the creek and she thought I had drowned. I went under the falls, was under there quite a while, scared her to death. Finally I broke through the falls and come out. She said, "Let's all go home." Now I was a leader and I was learning along with the girls, getting my badges alongside them. We would go to Star Lake Camp near New York City and then we'd go into the city to attend a commissioning. In the meantime we had a lot of free time and we would spend it going to places like the Empire State Building. Years later, my cousin Glad took me to New

York City and was so proud to show it to me because she wanted me to see the "other part of the world." I didn't tell her I had already been.

The Evangeline Residence sponsored by the Salvation Army was how I was introduced into the Army. The first Salvation Army meeting I ever attended was a funeral service for a lady who lived on the top floor at the Evangeline Residence. They told us to go into the chapel to the funeral and that was the first time I saw the insides of the church. I wasn't used to Army ways where they get up and tell about what people meant to them. The lady's son, Andrew Miller, told about his mother. Years later, I received a letter from him when he was a commissioner in the Salvation Army.

At that time, however, I was trying to make a choice. I had an offer to change my life, move out of Pennsylvania, and I feel the Lord wanted me to be strong in my choice by showing me all those different ways I could go in life, testing me to make sure I really wanted to follow His path.

2

*My help cometh from the* L<small>ORD</small>,

*which made heaven and earth.* **Psalm 121:2**

It all started on a sightseeing trip to Mammoth Cave in Kentucky. A few of us girls got our money together and convinced one girl's aunt to drive us there. Her aunt was stationed in Ohio, had cancer and wanted to go on over to North Carolina before she died to see a fellow Salvation Army officer, someone named Major Brown. Since we were that close already, we agreed. That's the day I met Major Cecil Brown, and that's when my life changed.

Major Brown changed a lot of lives there in the mountains through her mission. In the old days, there were circuit riding preachers that would come to the mountain people. They'd preach the word and go on to the next place, not doing any mission service, only preaching. Major Brown's mother for years had prayed for a preacher who would stay and minister to the people. She never had any idea the answer to her prayer would be her own daughter. People kind of step back when it's a woman preacher, but she was from around there and soon won their hearts.

With my friends, we had gone to see Max Patch, this patch of bald ground in the middle of all the tree covered mountains. It's a huge empty hill where no trees grow, where you can climb to the top and see for miles with no trees blocking your view. Now I go to

15

sunrise service there. There's nothing like seeing the sun come up over the mountains on Easter morning standing on Max Patch Bald. You know God exists.

But that day, as we were driving around as tourists, we went from there up the side of the mountain to Maple Springs Mission, all on dirt roads, by the way. This mission served the mountain people in the area helping them not only in a spiritual way, but also with food and medical supplies, even shelter for those who needed it. The major had started the mountain mission back before 1935 and it had grown bigger and bigger and she was needing more help. Major Brown picked me out and said to me, "Why don't you come here?" I didn't say anything, but to myself, I said, "not me." I didn't know where I wanted to go in life, but I didn't want to come back down here, not this far away. Besides that, I was a city girl by then, or at least I thought so.

The hug and the call to mission from Major Brown.

We had enjoyed our visit and we were ready to go back home. Major Brown's not one to hug people, but she gave me a big hug, held on to me and said for the second time, "I want you to come back and work for me."

I went in her yard there at Maple Springs, praying. I picked a frog up and played with it. I sat down playing with that frog and said,

"Oh, it's wonderful to see these trees." That's what I was raised up on in Fellsburg, but in the city in Pittsburgh, I did miss the trees. I missed the animals. Major Brown said it again, "Why don't you come down here and work?" I didn't say anything to her but I said it again in my mind, "Not me, not down in these mountains." I was in my early twenties, my whole life ahead of me. I had come to these North Carolina mountains from Kentucky just to visit, certainly not to move. At home in Pennsylvania, with the coal mines, the dirt was real rich and black. North Carolina had yellow and red clay and I couldn't believe the difference between the two. Yet I was so hungry. I fell in love with all these beautiful trees in North Carolina, even that frog in the yard.

The citadel at Maple Springs.

I didn't say anything to her at that time, but I went back to Pittsburgh and started thinking while the Lord started working on me about moving. Major Brown would send me a newsletter from her mission, but still I fought the idea of moving there. I wasn't even saved back then, yet Major Brown still wanted me. I guess God wanted me, too. In 1949 back in Pennsylvania I went to a camp meeting at the Salvation Army Camp Allegheny and that's where I was saved. It makes me think of Paul in the book of Acts. His conversion shook the daylights out of him and the Lord shook the daylights out of me at that camp meeting, too. Still I said, "Lord, I can't come down there. I just can't go," and the Lord just kept on and on.

My job at work wasn't going too well. They had a little trouble with the foreman at Joseph Horne & Company Department Store. Since I didn't belong to the union, I worked on through a strike and I crossed the picket line. Things got pretty bad and he got some of us to work on the floor, but I was not good at that. A customer came up and offered me a job as a bookkeeper at her store. I said "I don't know the first thing about that kind of work."

She says, "I'll teach you."

"No."

Another customer wanted me to work in her millinery store. "No, not interested." I know the Lord was dealing with me through that as well, showing me different paths.

I think the Lord sometimes tests us to make us be strong in the decisions that we make, because during those two years while I was fighting the Lord and not wanting to move, every boyfriend that I really liked turned up! I'd go out with them, then realize they weren't for me. I mean I dated a lot, but I didn't particularly care for any others, just went for fun of going out. But there were three special boys, these three I really kind of liked and they all showed up the summer I was making a decision about my future.

There was a boy stationed in the Air Force. He was an assistant editor of the paper although he was in the service, a sergeant. He'd come around to see me. I had a friend that was in the secret service and she worked there too. She came to see me one day and she said, "You know, he still talks about you."

Then a boy I had not seen for a long time, but I used to date in high school, he just showed up. We had a date.

A third fellow I hadn't seen in years was president of the Methodist camp. He came around and took me to the movie. I didn't know it, later I found out, but there was a girl in the Evangeline Residence and I wondered why she was offish toward me. All of a sudden I saw his picture on her dresser and I realized why.

I used to think when I was a youngin' my mother didn't do the right thing by getting a divorce. Back then you just didn't get divorced. It was wrong. I thought, well, if I never married, then I wouldn't have to worry about getting a divorce, because if I didn't like a fellow, I would kick him out. That's the attitude I had.

During this time I was like Jonah, trying to go the other way from where God asked me to go, though I wasn't exactly running away. I fought the Lord for two and a half years until I finally wrote to Major Brown and told her I was coming. That was after one day, over the top of the board where I was working, I saw a woman with a hat on walk past on the boulevard. I ran to see if she had on a Salvation Army bonnet. She didn't and I was so disappointed. I realized, "You've got it bad. You better go." In my letter I told Major Brown I wanted to come.

She wrote me back and said, "Sorry, I can't use you." That's when I really realized I was disappointed and it hurt me so bad. I think the Lord did that purposely to make me feel that I really wanted it.

Instead I tried joining the WAC's, the women's division of the US army. I was ten years younger looking than I actually was and the girl says, "You know you have to be twenty-one."

I said, "I am twenty-one." They didn't think so, and they said, "You come back when the captain here retires."

They'd usually never tell you at the Evangeline Residence if you got mail, but one day one of the ladies from the office said, "You've got a letter in the mailbox. You better open it and see." Major Brown had sent another letter.

"Please come on down."

The people at the residence knew about it and begged me not to go. They said, "You've got a job up here. You don't want to go down in those old mountains." But I did.

I had already made my decision to go when I wrote to Major Brown and told her I was coming. She wrote back, "Get right with the Lord, get your driver's license and come on down."

Since I didn't drive, I asked for help with getting my license. The fellow that helped me said, "You sure you haven't learned to drive before this?"

Then he said, "Let's go on a date." See, the Lord was testing me again. After three lessons, I passed and got my driver's license. He said, "I can't believe you could do that so fast."

"Well, the Lord's in a hurry for me to get down to those mountains."

I went to North Carolina alone by bus, arrived in June, 1951. That bus ride to North Carolina was another time God sent someone to watch after me. Captain Burchette, the one I traveled with on that trip to Mammoth Cave, went to the bus station to see me off. She had a friend who went along with us and when I got on the bus, he instructed the bus driver to watch after me and keep me up front to have a good eye on me. On the way down, it got real cold on the bus and there was a fellow in the next seat who put a coat over me. The bus driver stopped the bus on the side of the road and turned around and said to him, "What are you doing under those covers?"

He says, "I'm not doing nothing, just keeping her warm." The driver thought he was doing something else. He kept me in the front seat from then on, seeing that nobody got smart with me. See how good God was?

## 3

*He will not suffer thy foot to be moved:*

*He that keepeth thee will not slumber.* **Psalm 121:3**

I was twenty-five years old when I arrived at Maple Springs and in July I turned twenty-six. They already had a person at the mission named Lorraine, so they needed me to have a different name. Major Brown said, "We'll use your middle name," but I never had a middle name.

Since I had to change from Lorraine, I just used my mother's name, Jean. From that day in 1951 until I retired in 1991, I was Jean. Then with retirement I had to go back to the old name, Lorraine, because of social security and insurance. It was funny, though, when people would call on the telephone I'd know which one it was, family or somebody in the Army, because I would be Jean if it was the Army. I would be Lorraine if it was family. There are characters in the Bible with name changes, too. Saul changed to Paul, Abram to Abraham, and his wife Sarai to Sarah. So Lorraine to Jean wasn't all that unusual. It was a new beginning.

There were many changes I had to go through besides my name, learning to drive different to begin with. I had to have a driving lesson there first thing because they had a jeep and I'd never even been inside a jeep. It had a clutch, like cars back then, but that was all I knew about driving a jeep. Major Brown took me up one of the

21

mountains and said, "Now, you have to learn to drive again. Forget everything you've learned. I'm going to teach you to drive these mountains." And she did.

The Jeep.

She was always making me back the car to park no matter where I went, park the car facing out, especially when I visited at homes. "Why in the world do you want to back the car in all the time?" Sometimes it was convenient but I learned the real lesson one day when I went and backed in where I visited a lady. She was in an old house where they butchered hogs. I had heard them say that the doctor told her to go down to the river to get some yellow root and mix it with a little white lightning to use for a cure, but she got it twisted around and she mixed it with a lot of white lightning. She drank that mixture and she was high. When I knocked on the door, she came out with them two long, I mean long, butcher knives, two and a half feet long, not counting the handles. Ohhhh Brother! I had that car turned facing out and I went flying out of there. I never fussed again about Major Brown making me back the car to park it, and I still do it yet today.

She taught me some driving and then her nephew, Mickey Brown, taught me more. He's the one that taught me how to drive on ridges when we would go way back in the mountains where there'd be deep ruts in the road. The jeep was small and the wheels were narrow so we had to ride the ridges. The roads were just logging roads from where the log trucks would come along and make big gullies, not the main road, where they at least tried to keep a little gravel. These were the back roads, mostly dirt, the ones that went to the people's homes.

Another lesson I had to learn first thing was how to walk down the mountain. Remember now, we had skirts on as we were hiking across the mountain. Major Brown taught me there at Round Mountain where you had to swing on a rope along the river to get across. There was no way you could crawl, but you had to swing, almost hang on to the rocks and slide. The ropes were provided there because this was the Appalachian Trail, and we used the same section as the hikers. Seems like every part of my life I can find reflected in scripture, even something as simple as a hike. Isaiah 43, the first two verses: ...*Fear not: for I have redeemed thee, I have called thee by thy name; thou art mine. When thou passest through the waters, I will be with thee; and through the rivers, they shall not overflow thee*... I learned right away there was more in store for me at this mountain mission than a stroll down a rose covered walkway.

We walked past this one place where there were some barrels buried, sticking up about six inches out of the ground. I said, "Major, what's that?"

She laughed and said, "That's where they put their liquor." That was another lesson I had to learn first thing, moonshining in western North Carolina. A fellow took me around the mountains and told me that everywhere you see running water, you can trace it and there'll be a still. Major Brown never would do anything about people that had liquor. "When they get right with the Lord, they'll get rid of it."

There used to be kind of a swamp at the far end of the Salvation Army property. A moonshiner told me about one time a writer had written about some barrels of liquor he had hidden there. He spoke up and said yes, there was liquor hidden in the swamp, but, "That man wrote in the book that I had twelve barrels, and I only had seven." He didn't think about the part that he was telling on himself. But then he pointed at a building, said, "That right there was a liquor barn and that's where I got saved." When someone reported his still and the sheriff came, this same moonshiner would stand by, leave the doors unlocked so the law could look in. "As long as they're feeding their families," and the law would look the other way. When the revenuers came, that was different. If the bootleggers were down stream, their friends would dynamite the creek just to warn them. It made the fishermen mad, though, because it killed the fish.

There was a fellow that was the supervisor of all the men that worked on the road and Major Brown invited him in for dinner. I said, "Major, he's not coming with all his men. What's wrong?"

She said, "Aw, he's hiding his liquor because he knows I won't let it in the house."

He had white lightning, and to boot it all, one of our girls went and got it and kept it for medicine. One of the other girls got real sick one time, had the awfulest cold and she gave her a little bit of that stuff, knowing she would never have touched it if she knew it was liquor. She was awful sick, and she went to sleep. She woke up, "Give me some more." She gave her more and she went back to sleep. She said, "Aw, that medicine is so good, give me some more."

"No, I think you've had enough." She never to this day knew that was liquor, white lightning. Major Brown never knew either!

I learned how to spot white lightning for sale, too. When they wanted to sell it, they would get some kind of jug like a milk jug, hang it up in a tree. The handle part pointed where the liquor was. They would take the liquor and then there would be a rock nearby and they'd put the money under the rock. Honor system.

One day, Major Brown took me with her to visit a lady that the neighbors said needed help. They weren't that bad off although they reported them because the neighbors had looked at the house and thought they needed help. When we went in the yard, there were chickens everywhere. They had pigs running around, too. We went in the house and saw a pathway to the living room, and on both sides of this hallway, a pantry with its shelves from the ceiling down filled with corn meal, flour, sugar, liquor, everything they would need. Major Brown went in and she said, "I had a report that you folks were needing help."

"Some people know more about us than we do ourselves." The lady was laying down in the front room. There were two chairs there. One was kind of nice. The other one was plain, a frame around the chair with no seat at all, no cover, no nothing, just a frame. Major Brown sat down in the good seat and she said, "Jean, sit down on that seat." Brother, I sat on that broken down chair like it was just beautiful and after I left there, she quit teasing me! She said I caught on with what she was trying to teach me, to accept whatever comes.

Major Brown is the one that trained me on other things. Years later when I went to Winston-Salem, Major Dot Rickard said, "Yeah, when you were trained by Major Brown, you got trained." She was rough, whew. Made you walk the chalk line, too.

When they were working on the road building the interstate, there was a man, one of the supervisors, who came to the yard with a rifle. Now Major Brown was a crack shot, could hit the bull's eye every time, and he had heard about it. He wanted her to shoot, wanted to see it for himself. She didn't want to embarrass him so she'd shoot pretty close to the target, but not right on it. She said, "Why don't you shoot now?" He shot and didn't even hit the target.

I said, "Well, let me try it. Let me take my jacket off," so I handed it to him. I shot right at the target, hit the target, but not right on center, and I had never even shot before. When he started to put the coat back on, he started to give me a hug. He took one look at Major Brown and he pinched up the seams of that jacket at the shoulders, dropped the coat on me. After he left, Major Brown came to me, said that she realized it was just a wholesome hug and asked, "Am I too strict?" She was. Boy, you didn't look at a fellow when she was around. I says, "Yeah."

Open Air with Major Brown.

I watched her preach, hold open air meetings, hold Holiness Meetings, but she taught me just plain things mostly. She's the one, when I first went there, said, "I want you to go out and sweep the walk." I didn't know how to sweep the walk. I'd been in town, working in sewing, and never had the need to do something like that. I shoveled snow a little bit at the Evangeline Residence in Pittsburgh, but we were just having fun, didn't really do much shoveling. But now she told me to sweep the walk. I tried and when I came inside, my hands were in blisters.

Another time she said, "I want you to go down to the garden and hoe."

"Major Brown, I don't know how to hoe."

"Go down and hoe." So I did what she said.

She followed me down, but I didn't know it. I looked at the kids hoeing. I tried. I yanked a couple times.

Major said, "Go to the house."

"What did I do wrong?"

She said, "You was keeping all the weeds and pulling all the good stuff." I didn't know.

But if you would try, she'd be good to you. You had to go and do it, whether you knew how or not, and she was behind you to help. A fellow came through several years ago, Major Frank Duracher, collecting stories about Major Brown, talked to me and I told him that story and many others. He included right many of them in his book about her, *Smoky Mountain High, The Consuming Passion of Cecil Brown*, published it in 2007.

A visit to Major Brown's cabin where she grew up.

Another story I told him, Major Brown had told me to go the kitchen and make the corn bread. I never even ate corn bread, let alone made it. There was a wood stove and I didn't know how to build a fire in a cook stove, so I was guessing. When I was young, I had gone along with my cousin Glad and the Girl Scouts and learned how to make a fire, so that's how I tried to make the fire in that cook stove.

A little girl came in. I bet she was about in the fifth grade. "You don't know how to build a fire?" I just looked at her. She took all that wood out and fixed that fire right.

"Do you know how to make cornbread?" she asked me.

"No."

Then she mixed up the cornbread because I didn't know the first thing about it.

But that's the way Major Brown was. "Go try." She taught me how to make gingerbread. She took me down to the old cabin where she was raised and showed me how. I don't remember how to do it because I never did it after that, but she showed me how.

Another time Major Brown took me down to that cabin and I watched her nephew Mickey and her as they scrubbed the floor with lye soap. She got on the front porch and he got on the back porch. They both had a rifle. The lye soap brought out the rats and snakes. As they came out, they shot them.

I have several other stories about animals running wild. I was visiting at a house in nearby Cool Springs when a bunch of wild hogs came chasing me. I had to run and jump in the car so they wouldn't get me. Instead they got under the house.

Major took me where they were killing a pig. They cut all the insides out and as it hung, you could look inside the pig. It was so pretty and clean. I looked above on a porch and saw two women who were dressed real nice. Then just all of a sudden, they put their fingers up to their mouth and "Patooey." I was shocked to death. I had never seen women spit tobacco before, and Major Brown knew it. She didn't crack a smile, but her eyes were just dancing. She really enjoyed watching me.

Major Brown took me to Poplar Gap and sat me down on purpose beside a lady with a baby. It was right in the middle of the meeting when the woman decided she would feed the baby. My eyes got big. I didn't realize at first what Major Brown was doing. She was trying to get me used to everything, trying to break me in. Way back, people would nurse bare, without covering and I soon got used to that. Mountain women were tough, lived hard. They had a midwife that delivered babies all over this place. She couldn't read or write, but she'd deliver their babies. She knew all the herbs to make you well if you were sick. She had a baby herself and then went right out and hung her clothes out to dry.

As for food, that was another thing I had to adjust to. I didn't like their pinto beans, don't like them even yet today. I didn't like the green beans that they cook because they cooked them too much and with pork fatback. Some foods they had I really liked and enjoyed, but the others, I tried my best to gag them down.

I never had to cook, never learned how. If I ever cooked for people, they'd probably be dead! First my aunt that raised me wouldn't let me in the kitchen, so I didn't learn there. Then I lived in the Evangeline Residence and didn't have to cook. In North Carolina I didn't cook because of Blanche Lowe. She was the secretary and the cook, did all the cooking, and lived at the headquarters. Major Brown took her when she was just a young girl, sent her to school to learn secretarial work. She was a pretty good cook and Major Brown didn't want anybody else in the kitchen.

Once I tried to make coffee, didn't make it right. "Blanche, you didn't make this coffee, did you?"

"No, she did," and pointed straight at me.

"Don't let her make coffee any more. It tastes terrible." I didn't know she put a pinch of salt in the coffee to take the bitterness out.

Strange how things turn out. One day Major Brown said, "I want you to take Mickey down and get his driver's license." He's the one that taught me how to drive in the mountains, how to get cars out of ditches, how to pull them out of gullies and everything. I kept a tow chain all the time and if somebody was in a ditch, I'd get them out because he's the one that taught me how. He's also the one who knocked at the window early one morning, "Jean, would you help me get my car out? I went over the bank and I want to get it out before Aunt Cecil finds out about it." I went down there pulled the car out, never did tell Major Brown that part of the story.

But now she wanted me to go help him get his driver's license! He drove all the time, but he just drove around the mountain roads.

I said, "Mickey, have you ever driven on a paved road?"

He looked around and smiled. "No."

I said, "Listen, you're a good driver but before you get your license, let's go down to Frog Level in town and do some driving until you get used to the pavement." He was used to other cars coming at him, just wasn't used to that paved road. That day he drove up and down the paved road and I could tell he was getting used to it real quick like I knew he would. He got his license and he said, "I just want to thank you."

Mickey would teach me a lot of things about living in the mountains. When I would come back late in the evening, he would be the one who watched for me until I got home. I had four wheel drive and I would help people when they were stranded. Sometimes it would be midnight before I was coming home. I'd see people all over the road, off the mountain in little ditches, the fronts of their cars hanging off. I'd say to them, "What's the matter fellow? How about me pulling you out?"

They'd look at me, a woman, and so short at that. I was real little in size back then, a lot littler than I am now. "What'd you say?"

"I said, 'Let's get that car out of there. I've got a tow chain. You hang it under the springs.'" Some cars don't have much bumper and you have to put the chain under the supports down under the car. "I'll pull you out. Go on." So they'd do it and I'd pull them out.

"Whew, thank you. I never thought you could do that."

I was twenty-six and they thought I was sixteen because I looked a lot younger than I was. They didn't recognize me as being older until my hair turned gray.

There was a fellow that had a big trailer and he was going down toward Lake Junaluska, going all over the road, having a hard time controlling it in the ice and snow.

"How about me pulling that trailer for you?"

"What?"

"Let me pull that trailer for you."

So I towed it down to where there was a safe place and he says, "We'll leave it up in there and then when the weather clears, come back for it." He was scared. He was scared of me too, I think.

He says, "What do I owe you?"

I says, "The next time you see the tambourine, put some money in it." Do you know what? He ran a business that sold alcohol, where customers drank, like at a bar. When I would go in, he'd put a dollar in the tambourine. Every time. 2 Corinthians 9:7 says *So let each one give as he purposes in his heart, not grudgingly or of necessity; for God loves a cheerful giver.* He realized the Salvation Army does something and he gave willingly.

The Lord made a way for me to be accepted by the people there, too. There are plenty of scriptures in the Bible instructing the people of Israel on hospitality to strangers. Ephesians 2:19 *Now therefore ye are no more strangers and foreigners, but fellow citizens with the saints, and of the household of God*; and Leviticus 19:34 *But the stranger that dwelleth with you shall be unto you as one born among you, and thou shalt love him as thyself; for ye were strangers in the land of Egypt: I am the LORD your God.* Here in this mountain mission the people took those Bible verses to heart, accepting and appreciating and learning from me even though I was a stranger.

I had to adapt to so many changes when I first arrived in the mountains of North Carolina, but most of all, it was the language.

Striking a picture with friends.

They spoke old English. I spoke Pennsylvania Anglo Saxon. We had to use sign language. Of course they talked with everything drawled out, the slow southern drawl. Yankee people, one reason why they're not accepted here, is because they talk so fast the mountain people think they're mad at them.

They'd say things like, "Up air." I didn't know they were saying "Up there." At the trading post, we had a little store and a fellow came who wanted a dope. Shocked, I said, "What did you say?"

"A dope," he said again.

Major Brown heard us. "You jarhead, give him a Coca Cola." I didn't know dope was a mountain word for soda. Dope meant drugs to me, even back then.

They had other ways of saying things, too. Once this lady was in the garden and she wanted pictures made with a camera, "I's want you to stay long enough for the boys to get down here so we can strike your picture with them."

I tried every way to communicate with them. When they wanted me to do something, they'd just use sign language to tell me what to do. It was really terrible. They made fun of me and I thought I would never fit in. Finally I said to Major Brown, "Major, when am I going to be accepted as a mountaineer?"

At a meeting in front of some people from headquarters, she gave me a little slip of paper that says something about a person that learns to talk our language and learns to eat our food becoming one of us. She signed it and whole bunch of them did too and she said, using my Army name, "Jean's from the mountain now. You're accepted." When they gave me that little certificate, the recognition, they gave me a bouquet of flowers and said, "She had a little bit of a culture shock."

I said, "Yeah, from Pittsburgh, Pennsylvania to Max Patch," and the place roared laughing.

To Whom It May Concern
This is to certify that Jean Lorraine Frese
Having met the qualifications, is now a 100%
"MOUNTAINEER."
She is to be no longer looked upon as a
"FURRINER."
To reach this high state of perfection, a "Yankee"
must be willing
To speak our language,
Eat of our Rations,
And love it.
Signed this the 29th day of July, 1951
Major Cecil Brown and friends.

# 4

*Behold, He that keepeth Israel*

*shall neither slumber nor sleep.* **Psalm 121:4**

People are the same all over the world, through all the years from Bible times down to now. What was evil then, is evil now, and William Booth, the man who founded the Salvation Army in the 1850's knew that. He lived in London, England and saw poverty and hunger. He saw thieves and prostitutes, gamblers and drunken fathers spending money on evils rather than on family. Same as every where. We had all that in the mountains, and bootleggers, too. I've known people to take a woman and use her body to make money. The husband would rent her out to get his liquor. They didn't have love, only used her for what he wanted.

I once took a little girl to the doctor. "I've never seen a child so illiterate," the doctor told me.

Major Brown had said I wouldn't be able to get her away from the family, but to go ahead and try. The grandmother had her at her house and when I got there, I found her on a dirt floor. This girl didn't know a thing because they didn't teach her at all, never had gone to school.

We got her straightened out, started feeding her and she started developing into a lady. Her mother came to visit her and saw that she was growing. She wouldn't bother her when I was nearby, but when I went on vacation, she slipped in, took her back and the girl went wild. London or North Carolina, no difference.

William Booth was a Methodist minister in England and got this urgency to serve those people who did not know the Lord, those that would not feel welcome or comfortable in the churches of that time. He decided to go out in the world to them, to feed them, help them get back on their feet and send them to church. But the churches didn't welcome them, so he opened a place for them to meet where they could minister to each other and study the scriptures.

It became officially The Salvation Army, organized with a military kind of structure. The general is the leader, supported on down the line by commissioners, brigadier generals, colonels, lieutenant colonels, majors, captains and lieutenants. His daughter, Eva Cory Booth, was the National Director for the United States Salvation Army for thirty years and she was General over it all from 1934 until 1939. She was better known as Evangeline, and the Evangeline Residence where I lived in Pittsburgh was named for her.

The Salvation Army prepares its soldiers for a war. It's a real war with a real enemy, evil. Its soldiers are the converts that enlist as Salvationists. Those who feel called to become officers enter a cadet training period and then apply to be ordained and become commissioned officers beginning with the rank of lieutenant. They could be preachers, teachers, social workers, counselors, youth leaders and musicians, any one of those jobs, or mostly all those jobs at the same time.

Noncommissioned local officers help some too, often working with youth. Officers live in quarters and drive vehicles provided by the Army. They wear uniforms and when they salute, it's not to higher ranking officers, not even to the general, but only to God by pointing upward, toward heaven. The Army has commissioners all over the world. It's during the commissioner meeting that they come to London and select the general.

Starting in 1949 in Pittsburgh I was a soldier in the Army. I became an Auxiliary Captain in December 1961. I went through officer's training and was commissioned in 1973 as Captain and by the time I retired I was a Major.

The Army had rules and strict expectations from its very beginning. For example, Salvationists have to abstain from alcohol, drugs and tobacco. Major Brown was strict with us, too, would not allow me to talk to a man by myself in case he would get the idea that I was in love with him. Showing emotion could not happen.

The Army provided my uniforms to me at what it cost to make. When I first came, it was a navy blue dress with a pleat down each side, full skirt and high collar, I mean, a real high collar. We had white uniforms, too, back then, and I also had a gray uniform. General Booth's wife Catherine designed the bonnet that we wore, the one that tied over to the side, based it on a poke bonnet, the style that was popular in England at that time. We wore our bonnets on Sundays and I also wore it to collect. Oh, hot as everything.

In my white uniform at a Home League gathering.

Now the Salvation Army doesn't use bonnets, only hats, but a lot of people in the corps don't wear even hats. In fact, some of them don't wear a uniform.

Sometimes wearing a uniform backfires. Years ago Brigadier Henry was coming down the mountain and came upon some boys who were doing something against the law and had wrecked. When they saw Brigadier in his uniform, they thought he was the law. They climbed trees to get away and he was only trying to help them.

You understood when you become part of it all, they don't give you much salary. Good benefits back then, though. Officers live in quarters provided by the Army, not paying rent. Their work place is headquarters, the main church, usually the place where things first began. It's called the citadel and the individual churches are the corps. Maple Springs was the citadel when I first arrived. We had about four corps and later Shelton Laurel became the citadel.

Maple Springs was where I lived the first six years after I moved to North Carolina. I actually lived in Haywood County and ate in Madison County because the line went right through the middle of the property. In the front of the Citadel was a church and at the back, the dining room and living quarters. In the wintertime we ate at a big round table in the citadel, but in the summertime we had small round tables outside near a field. Out in the back we had a spring house near the creek where we stored food since we didn't have a refrigerator. Major Brown told me about a time someone stole food from there. They took it home and then they had the nerve to invite her to dinner. She was eating her own food.

Waiting outside the dining room.

One other time Major Brown noticed that she was losing a lot of food out of the spring house. She said to us, "All right, I want you all to leave. I'm going to slip back and I'm going to hide in the upstairs of the citadel." She had her rifle and went up to my room in the back of the main building where you look out at the spring house. When they came to steal the food, she shot over their heads. She said, "They won't come back no more." She never lost any more food there.

Major Brown also had what she called the hillside house. Some folks would sleep there, like extra rooms available when someone needed them. People would be hiking on the Appalachian Trail and sleep overnight there since the trail went through up there at the spring.

There also used to be a wash house, called the "bird house" and when they got an overload of people, they had to go in there to sleep. In winter, they about froze to death. When they put curlers in their hair, rolled it and wet it, their hair froze. It was that cold.

Major even sent me to weaving school at Penland to learn a profession. I made cloth to use for sewing clothes for the kids there at the mission. She had a big loom in the trading post where people could make rugs to sell and earn money. I didn't do too much weaving, but I did it some while she was trying to find something for me, something that fit me.

She found it. I started working with the children.

We kept children, built a house for them next door to the church, Haywood House, where the children lived. It wasn't an orphanage, not exactly. Those children, maybe they were children whose parents were getting a divorce and having to decide where each child would go. Some children, their parents were having trouble and they were taken away from their home. And then some of them were just

In my room at Haywood House.

pitiful, mistreated at home. One tried to burn the schoolhouse down, but they didn't want to put him in jail because he was too young. So he came to us.

The law didn't want these children to go to an orphanage or a place like that because for the most part they would only have minor problems. Haywood House was not funded except for what we could collect. We had to go out and bring in the money and if we didn't, we'd just have to eat less. It wasn't often that we couldn't get enough money, happened a couple times.

Somebody once wanted me to watch their children while they were gone. "I can't watch children. The only kind of children I know how to do is troubled children. I wouldn't know what to do with regular children." I could handle troubled children easy, the ones I was trained to do. You know the Lord doesn't always give you a chance to know what you do at the time. You just have to do it by faith.

I've had children that came up on the mountain to live at Maple Springs and they'd be up there two years or so. Years later they'd see me and tell me that's the only happiness they ever had as a child, those two years they were there. Then you know what you did.

I took care of these children. I sewed clothes for them, became like a mother. Major Brown even made me give them castor oil when they needed it. Those poor kids didn't like it one bit, but she said they needed to be cleaned out once a year.

The ones that lived at the home went to school on the bus that picked them up at Haywood House. But see, there were other children who lived way back in the mountains with their families. They couldn't get to the bus early in the mornings, so we created a school for them. It was started by Lieutenant Florence Wall who taught the children the first two years. She left and that's when I took over to teach them. They were darling, sweet, and they couldn't get away with anything because I had already done it myself.

The school was in the upstairs of the trading post at Maple Springs. Major Brown's office was off to one corner downstairs and we had a little place to sell snacks to people. There was stairs, long stairs sort of like attic stairs leading up to where we had the school room. Major Brown had gotten some old desks that the schools had discarded. The public school gave us the textbooks or else we just used what we could get. Blanche Lowe fixed lunch for us and we'd go over there to the citadel and eat.

One morning it was time for school and we were in the trading post ready to go upstairs. I opened the door and ah, the odor that came down to me. I yelled up, "What in the world is that smell?"

"Well, Miss Jean, there was a poor little old skunk that was stuck in a hole in the log. And we couldn't leave it stay there. We had to help it out."

They helped it out all right. I says, "Well, children, school's out today. Go home and wash in tomato juice."

When I was in the drug store one day the druggist asked me to read something for him and I couldn't read it. I thought, "Brother, you better learn to read." I went back to the old ways my aunt taught me to skip the words. She told me if you don't know a word, read past and then come back and you can about guess what it was. That's how I learned how to read and that's how I taught them to read.

I learned right along with them, taught them things that I didn't learn, that I had to learn after I got out of high school. See, when I was growing up, I'd do everything I could to keep from working. I wouldn't turn work in, even when I knew the answer. The other kids felt so bad for me sometimes they would give me pieces of paper with the answers on them. Oh, I knew all the tricks and so these children couldn't pull any on me.

I taught school there for two years. I had four grades, only one classroom, and six students, sort of like home schooling today. Those children kept me busy, but they learned and they could read fluently, all of them. I taught them how to spell, too. I never did learn to spell so I was learning along with them. I figured if they never went to school anymore, at

Salvation Army Trading Post with school room on top floor.

least I taught them to read and I taught them to add and subtract, do things that are necessary in life. They would know their money, know how much they had and nobody could trick them. When they went to public school after those years, two of them skipped a grade and one of them skipped two grades. The teacher said they were the politest children in the whole school, couldn't believe it. They weren't fancy dressed, either, but they were neat.

At Maple Springs we had the schoolhouse and the trading post, Haywood House where the children lived, the main building where we held meetings and smaller ones out back. Major Brown had another house she would use for the divorced people, women who had domestic problems and needed to get away.

So there I was in the mountains. Teaching. Working with children. Going into homes to bring the Bible and the word of God. Hard work. But I watched Major Brown, others, too and noticed something about them. They were different from me. They had like a radiance about them. It was something they had that I was lacking and I set out to find what it was.

I asked what was the difference, what did they have that I didn't, and they told me. They had been sanctified, made holy, received the

Holy Spirit just like John the Baptist spoke about in Matthew 3:11, *I indeed baptize you with water unto repentance, but He that cometh after me is mightier than I, whose shoes I am not worthy to bear: He Himself will baptize you with the Holy Spirit and fire.*

I was baptized in a Methodist Church in Pittsburgh. I was raised in church, but I would sit there and I would count the blocks in the wall and not listen. When I was grown, I went to a camp in Pennsylvania and during a meeting there, this boy was so anxious for me to get right with the Lord, but he was being persistent, turning me off. The preacher went up to him, said, "Stop, don't do that. You push people and they'll say no. It will make them harder. Don't shout religion on people." I found that out through the years because of that experience. If they say no, I don't talk to them much. I'll just tell them my life story. When I got saved, I was again at the same camp.

I knew that I knew the Lord after that, but there was still something wrong, something more, something they had that I didn't. So I prayed, "Lord, how can I explain it to teach people when I don't even know it myself? There's another experience beyond being saved. I don't know how to explain it to them." The Lord answered me, brought it to me.

I figured out it's like the credit card. When you're saved, you have the Holy Spirit in you, but it's not activated. You get a credit card and until you call on the telephone and activate it, it's no good. That's the same way with people. If they don't let the Holy Spirit in their hearts, it doesn't do them any good. They've got it, but what good is it? I hadn't activated it.

When a person gets sanctified, that lets the Holy Spirit work in their lives and gives them more power. Peter was just an old fisherman, but through the Holy Spirit, he was preaching and won many souls for the Lord. Peter, the fisherman Jesus called to be one of his disciples. Peter, that old fisherman, the one changed because of the Holy Spirit, the one who was present on that day of Pentecost when the Holy Spirit came upon the multitudes. Acts 2:2 says, *And suddenly there came a sound from heaven as of a rushing mighty wind, and it filled all the house where they were sitting.*

I talked to one girl that I knew had the Holy Spirit. She didn't have to tell me because I could feel it on her. You just know because the spirit reveals it to you. I talked to her about it and she said, "Well, I got sanctified."

"How?"

But she says, "I just accepted it." No proof. It has happened to some people at the same time as being saved, when lots of people figure they get the Holy Spirit, and sometimes they do. That didn't happen to me. I couldn't do that. I wanted proof. I was like Gideon in the sixth chapter of Judges asking God for proof. He put out a fleece and if it was wet by the dew and all the ground around it was dry, that would be his proof that God would save Israel by his hand. When that happened, he wanted more proof, asked it again, only backwards, for the fleece to be dry and all the ground around it wet. It happened, and then he believed. He needed proof, and I did, too.

I talked to others and I could tell they had the Holy Spirit. I knew it. They witnessed to me, not saying it, but I knew it. There was a lady at headquarters, a young woman. They were having a program and I looked at all the young ladies at headquarters and she stood out among the bunch. I didn't even know her at the time, but I knew that woman was sanctified. She's a lieutenant colonel, retired now, Lt. Col. Jean Mikles. She just radiated. I knew she was sanctified.

I could tell Major Brown had something more than what I had, too. Once I saw her sleeping on the couch with this beautiful smile on her face, like a heavenly smile. When she woke up, I said, "You know, you have such a beautiful smile."

She said, "A lot of people have told me that."

I said to her, "Major Brown, I love the Lord and I know I'm saved, but I'm losing out somewhere and I don't understand what's wrong. I don't want to have religion that I don't understand."

She said, "You need to find the Holy Spirit. I know where you can go to get it."

She sent me to Kentucky Mountain Holiness Association camp meeting at the Wesleyan Armenian camp in Van Cleve, Kentucky. The founder, Lela McConnell, had graduated at nearby Asbury College. I attended the camp meeting a couple years, a few weeks at a time, and I got to where I thought I wasn't even saved. It bothered me so bad. I'd take the horse and go in the woods and just ride. I tried to do it on my own, find the Holy Spirit. It just drove me crazy. I knew I was doing things wrong. I tried to set it right, so I'd ask for forgiveness. I couldn't understand what was wrong.

Folks would tease me about going to the camp. They'd say, "Better watch out. You're so little, when they start shouting, they're gonna stomp all over you." I went up beside a lady and she started shouting and scared me half to death. I was afraid.

The second year I went, I was driving over the streetcar tracks near Mt. Carmel headed to the Kentucky Holiness Association and the car started sliding. I couldn't control the car from slinging back and forth. Just a voice out of nowhere said, "Take your foot off the brakes." That's the first thing I had done, put on the brakes. I couldn't believe what I heard. The voice said it again. "Take your foot off the brakes." I did and the car started straightening up. Got along a piece and it started sliding again and I put my foot on the brakes. This voice came again, "Take your foot off the brakes." I found out when I got there at the camp meeting they had been praying at that exact time for safety for all the people coming.

There was a lady come staggering down the stairs. "Oh, that's terrible. That's not proper in church." That's what I was thinking. She passed out. Some people ran to help her and asked me, "Why didn't you help that lady?" She was having a seizure, but I didn't know it. I thought she was in the spirit.

When I went to the camp meeting at Mt. Carmel the third time, Elma Reed, a schoolteacher there at Mt. Carmel school, stuck with me and prayed me through it. She never lost patience with me, prayed for me. I finally got sanctified and got the proof I was looking for.

"Lord I want proof," I said, and the Lord gave it to me. Proof came to me and I believed. It was when finally I went up to the altar and I asked the Lord to sanctify me. "Lord," I says, "Lord, I know I'm saved. What's wrong with me? I can't figure it out."

I was very quiet and just all of a sudden, I raised my hand and shouted, "Thank you, Jesus!" I'd never used that word before. I would never say the word "Jesus" because all the times I ever heard it used, it was a cuss word, for cursing. Instead I would always say "Lord," but this time I said, "Thank you, Jesus," and I raised my hand. I had never, never shown any emotion. I was taught we were supposed to be quiet.

Just then, about half way up the steps I heard this whoooosh. Like that, whoooosh. No one else heard it, but I heard it. It wasn't loud, like it said it was in the Bible. It was shhhh. I could even see the direction it was coming from. Down the stairs, shhhh. That was proof to me. That was the Holy Spirit. Everything that I said when it happened were things I would never think of saying or doing without the Holy Spirit. That was my proof.

Shhhhhhhwwwweeehhhh. And what I did, I wanted to answer the Lord. I had read about the Lord and the Holy Spirit coming like a mighty rushing wind. And it went Shhhhhwwwweeeehhhh, like that to me. It was a mighty rushing wind.

I praised the Lord and the Lord's blessed me ever since then. He gave me the power to really preach, whereas before, I was preaching, but in a different way. The Lord started giving me things to say. I'd come up with things that I didn't even think about saying. It wasn't me. It was the Spirit.

For a long time after that, I never testified to it in the church. Finally I testified and I told about what had happened to me in the basement of the building at the camp, the place where they had built an altar. Before, I was scared and shy, had never testified. Never. But this time, Brigadier Henry and Major Clark and my friend, Sybil Wilburn and I had gone to a meeting and they asked for testimonies. I gave my testimony for the first time. Elma Reed, the one who had worked so hard to help me was there also. Once I testified, she shouted, tickled her to death so much, shouted because she was thrilled. The change for me was not being shy anymore. I used to be so shy about everything. The Holy Spirit gave me boldness like in scriptures, in the book of Acts, the boldness of the folks.

I was never ashamed after that to bow my head in a restaurant. The Lord led me to it, helped me through it. Even now, I go up to people in restaurants that said the blessing, talk to them, say, "I'm so proud to see you thank the Lord." It would kind of tickle them and they'd be thrilled. I admired one fellow one day because it was a bunch of fellows there and he was the only one that bowed his head and prayed. I talked to him. "I'm proud of you."

To show you how much I changed, look at the way I was when I was a child. My aunt sent me to the store, told me to get a loaf of bread. I could remember the loaf of bread, but I was just too shy to ask for it when I got there. She'd have to write it down on paper, I was just that shy. People say, "What happened to you now? You talk too much." Before I preach, I get nervous but after I get up there, I'm okay. I can do the Lord's mission because I'm sanctified.

Anything I do now for God, it's not from me. This is not me. It's the Holy Spirit in me.

5

*The Lord is thy keeper:*

*The Lord is thy shade upon thy right hand.* **Psalm 121:5**

I was sanctified after I had been in North Carolina about six years and from then on, I believed I could do all things through Christ who strengthened me. I sure needed that strength, because the mountain mission field was hard, wasn't for the faint of heart.

The church at Shelton Laurel was my first place as a preacher. Up to then I had worked at Maple Springs doing whatever was needed. When Major Brown told me to take it over, I said, "Major, I've never preached. I don't know anything about taking care of a church."

She says, "If you don't, I'm going to shut it down." They were going to close that little church if I didn't take it, and so I said, "Well, I can't do worse," and so I went.

Shelton Laurel is where Major Brown's mountain mission work actually started back in 1932, although it wasn't commissioned until a couple years later. Raymond Rathbone donated the land for the mission, but the major needed a building. They took an old schoolhouse from over in the silver mine that they weren't using any more, got permission to move it to Shelton Laurel to use for the church building. They just brought the whole building over and set it down and built on it.

Easter at Shelton Laurel.

By the time I first came in the mid-fifties, there were three of us in the church and I was one of the three, the other two, a husband and wife. With their help we built it up to forty-five, a good number for in the mountains. When I'd preach, I'd ask the Lord to help me. I'd just tell the people how I felt about the Lord. It's strange, the Lord sort of gets ahead, knows it's going to happen. I'd get a message, hear something, read something, and "You know, that would be a good message." Sometimes when I was doing my devotions, I'd write in the back of my devotion book things that would be a good topic for a sermon. I'd write notes down, but the notes seemed like they would just disappear once I started talking. The mountain people don't like the preacher using notes, very much against them. Now that things are a little bit more modern, they are kind of used to notes so I do use notes, but only to check down to see if I got everything said.

"You don't think we're going to go to heaven, do you?"

I'd say, "I don't judge you. God's the one that judges you. You have to answer to him." Of course, I had to learn the hard way, too, so I understood them.

This big, fancy car drove up one day, looked almost like a limousine, had a license tag, "Texas." This boy came up with a western cowboy hat. He said, "I'm going to marry you."

"You don't know me."

"Yes, I do. I do know you." He said, "I want to marry you."

I said, "Well, I'm not interested in marrying right now." We were in a meeting and there was a bunch of people around. He walked in that door and kissed me on the forehead. I started to go back a little. I heard someone say, "Who is that?" I even had to ask somebody who he was. Here, come to find out, it was a man whose mother I had been visiting all the time. This was their son, but I didn't even know his name. He come up and "I'm gonna marry you."

No.

The mountain folks, way back when I first got here, had to move away to get jobs. Some went to Michigan. This one went to Texas.

It was rough financially back in those days, not much way to make a living for the mountain folk, not much left over for the church. I had a fellow that knew someone that would give him carpet for the floor and build nice seats for pews at Shelton Laurel. The people of the church had been giving money or honoring somebody in the church by donating. We had all but the seven dollars and we couldn't order the pews until we had all the money collected. Can you believe it, I just hung the phone up from talking with this fellow and the phone rang. A lady called. She lived in a trailer, didn't have much money, but she called and says, "I understand you need seven dollars to get the seats for the church. I'll give that seven dollars." Just right there. Talk about God working.

I called the fellow right back up and said, "I got the seven dollars."

"You can get your pews." God works miracles. That was in the fifties and we've still got the same carpet on the floor and the same pews, although one of the officers after I left put padding on them.

We had visiting preachers come in once in a while. The Army will pay for one week of the messages, but one year this revival continued for three weeks, that long. The preacher said, "Don't worry about it. You can take an offering up and I'll just accept that." Can you believe it, those people ganged up and worked and got the money for the second week. We didn't have enough for the third week, and a man got in the back of the church and stood beside me and they just piled money in my hand. "Here, take this." It made enough to pay for three weeks revival. See? God works miracles. In fact, the whole mountain mission was a miracle continuing on from the work started years before by Cecil Brown.

The Salvation Army wanted to do a film about her and her work at the mountain mission. Captain Ivy Waterworth and Lt. Col. G. A.

Stephan created a movie, named it *Shepherdess of the Hills*. A film crew came in 1955 and filmed at Maple Springs. I acted her part in several scenes that showed when she first began the mission, when she was younger. People often thought that Major Brown was my mother, we looked that much alike, so it was natural for me to do that role. The film showed Haywood House and the children. It showed the Salvation Santa truck we used at Christmas to deliver presents to the children throughout the mountains. It also showed me playing the organ, which I don't. That was the only time in the filming that I was uncomfortable.

Major Brown retired from the army in 1956. She was actually young, but she was dying of cancer, promoted to glory in 1958. She had watched after me during those years I was with her, took care of me. I appreciated all she did in my life and I felt that the best way to honor her was to continue her work.

I was at Shelton Laurel and we had built the church up to about forty in attendance. Brigadier Henry, Major Brown's replacement, told me they were going to transfer me since they thought an officer should be in charge of this new church building, and see, I wasn't an officer at that time. So they moved me, sent me to Poplar Gap.

I had a wonderful time there at Poplar Gap because the people supported me all the way. I felt like they accepted me because they had loved Major Brown. I really loved them and the Lord just blessed me. One lady told me that when I prayed, she'd think Jesus was sitting right there with us in the chapel.

Actually the building at Popular Gap was just a shack, had oil lights that we'd burn 'cause we didn't have any electricity, had metal behind them to reflect more light. The people would come walking in with lanterns that

Poplar Gap.

we hung from the ceiling and they would get up on the platform with those lanterns, then go to singing. We didn't have bathrooms there, either, not even an outhouse, just a bush out back. It was all wilderness.

One girl had Rocky Mountain Spotted fever. I didn't know she was so desperately sick and I said, "Well, after church, I'll take her," and she died in the hospital. There was a bug, a tick, bit her, killed her. Like I say, wilderness.

There were two boys living near Poplar Gap. They would come down to the fence near the church, but when they saw me coming, they'd run. Every time I'd be there, they'd run away. "Ho, ho, ho. Wait a minute. Why don't you come into church?"

"No, no, no, no." Until finally, "I'll go," and they came in. They both got saved. One of them had the power to touch people. When he touched them, the young people, and old, too, they would go running to the altar and get saved. The other one had a brother that had been so mean to him, said, "One of these days, I'm gonna come out and get you, brother," and he did. He had a knife and he cut him all to pieces and he had to be put in the hospital.

Another man that got saved there quit drinking and his buddies didn't like it. It hurt them, caused trouble between them. We were having a revival with Major Abernathy, who was very little in size, and one of those buddies came. He said, "I'm gonna take that preacher and I'm gonna throw him against that wood stove."

This man I'm talking about that had found the Lord, very quietly went up to him, took one hand and put it in the back of his neck at his collar, took the other hand and put it on his belt, picked him up and very quietly took him outside and set him down very easy. "You don't do that here."

Then after that, we had another revival and this buddy was saved. He came down the aisle and I just couldn't believe it. It was unreal. The Lord just wonderfully blessed me. I went to the lowdownest church there was, where there was nothing, and that church gave me wonderful blessings.

When the lumber companies were up here in the mountains and had a lumber camp, the companies would put up a church to keep the loggers from being so rough. As they closed down, the people started moving away to get jobs, so the church was no longer used. That brought about the end of Poplar Gap, but we'd still have big groups come to special events like Singing on the Mountain when we'd have thousands of people show up.

I was moved to Little Creek when Poplar Gap closed, traveling across the mountain many a day on my newest assignment. I became an Auxiliary Captain on December 26, 1961 while I was stationed there at Little Creek. The letters I got from different officers said the promotion was "in recognition of your deep devotion and dedication to the work of the Army in the mountain mission."

It was work, believe me.

I worked a lot with youth at Little Creek, but I went to one of the older folks and I said, "Don't you want to go have prayer with us?"

He said, "Oh, I thought it was just for the young people." That's when I realized I was paying a little too much attention to them and leaving out the older people. I began working more with the older people, too, but not letting the younger people go. Most people want to work with young children, say about twelve, thirteen. Seems like I was better with people eighteen to twenty-five. They started coming to the church and to the prayer meetings before the regular meetings.

Music and Worship at Little Creek.

The mountain people were not book educated, but still they were eager to learn and I had to speak in a way they could understand. In the Bible times, religion was all rules and the regular people didn't understand it as well. The Lord did his preaching in parables because the people understood better. He had to bring it down to what they understood, just like I did.

I would go and pick up those people that had to go across the mountain, took me an hour to get them, take them to church. This one girl that was riding with me in the station wagon one day says, "I just feel like I want to find the Lord right now."

So I pulled the station wagon off the road and I took the front seat and folded it up and I says, "Well, here's your altar." She got down right there in the wagon and accepted the Lord as her Savior. She had lipstick on and she said, "I don't think I'm supposed to wear this lipstick any more." She took a Kleenex and wiped it off her mouth.

Another day when we were collecting, riding in the car, this woman with me, all of a sudden out of the blue, says, "Whooo, Glory, hallelujah."

I says, "What's happened?"

She says, "Now I know what you're talking about when you talk about sanctification." She got the Holy Spirit there in the car at Lake Junaluska.

One time this fellow, a bootlegger, got mad at another. He says, "I'm going to take you and I'm going to knock you out."

The other said, "Well, let's wait until after church and we can do this outside."

Somehow he got away and got home safe, but the next Sunday, his father showed up at church with a switchblade knife. When that knife was closed, it was as big as a butcher knife! I had never seen one that big. He said, "I ain't going to let nobody touch my son."

The son told me later, "I don't know what Daddy would have done if you hadn't took that knife off him. I didn't want him to hurt somebody."

I was taking a shortcut back home one day and ran off the road near Cherokee. Usually I could take one of those big long jacks and pump the car up and push it back on the road, but it was too far in. Three men come out of the woods. One got in the front, two in the back, lifted the car up and set it on the road. I turned around to thank them and they were gone. I was telling my friend Sib Wilburn about it years later and she said, "Did you ever think it was angels?" I didn't at the time, but I did after that because those men just disappeared.

There was a little shack above the church at Little Creek where I used to stay on nights I didn't want to drive back home across the mountain. Boss' wife worried about me staying up there all by myself, but it was safe. In fact, I enjoyed being by myself. A fellow that was hiking the Appalachian trail nearby the church came up to me once and he says, "I spent the night at your house. I cleaned out the fireplace for staying."

I drove those back roads so much that I wore cars out since it was rough going. One time I needed a new car but the Salvation Army didn't have money to buy one. I told them and told them I needed a replacement and they just wouldn't pass it. One of the headquarter fellows came up and I took him to one place on my circuit, Bonnie Hill, all dirt road, terrible going. When he went back I got a phone call. He said, "I want you to get a new car."

When I went up to the car dealership to get it I said, "Where do you want me to park this old car?"

"Just let it sit there." I had it parked in front where the cars come in. He said, "Leave it there, we'll move it after while."

When I went back there to see him later, he said, "How did you get this car up here?"

"A wing and a prayer."

He says, "You know what? We had to tow it off. The transmission fell out right here in the parking lot." Talk about the Lord taking care of you, that's close calling.

Another time the police stopped me even though I hadn't done anything bad. They said, "Tell your boss to get you some tires." Those tires were bald. That's where I got these bad knuckles, changing tires. Every time I had a flat tire, the Lord just was so good to me, always let me plop completely down right in front of a house. One time I had three flat tires at the same time, they were that worn out. It was on a dirt road and the tires were so thin. A man came out and fixed two of them and I used the spare tire for the other one, went on into town and got it taken care of.

I went by horseback, too, where there were no roads. I rode my horse, Chigger. My dress was long enough to ride with a saddle, so I didn't wear pants. I'd say to this one man, Ernest Presnell, "If you would saddle my horse, I could go down and have Sunday school for the children back in the mountains."

With my horse, Chigger.

This one particular family had a bunch of kids, about ten. The father drank. He was supposed to be hunting, but he got drunk, him and a bunch of others, and the building they were in burnt down. His dog dragged him out and he was burnt real bad, but the rest of them were killed. He was in terrible pain and Major Brown would send me to him to give him morphine shots. She said, "I'll teach you how to do it." She was going to use an orange, but I never did see that orange. She showed me only one time and I had to do it after that. The fellow was shocked I could give him the shot. He said, "Boy, you don't hurt."

I would teach Bible lessons in their house, made it so the children could understand. After a while I would have people that couldn't read and write coming. "You explain it so I can understand" and they weren't embarrassed to ask questions. In a church building they were. But with me in a house, they'd ask questions and they learned a lot. I would have almost as many in that little house that would be at the church just because people would come and feel at ease.

I taught those Sunday School children, rode Chigger to their house. The Lord blessed me there. When I was taking some books down to them one day, I thought there was an animal after me. The horse was wiggling her ears too much. "Someone's following me." Looked real quick. Someone jumped back in the bush, but I knew who it was. Next time I saw this man, I said, "Did I get I too close to your still?" He got so mad at me, he tried to kick the glass out of my lights in my car.

On my way to Sunday School.

He came back later and apologized. Now this same man's wife died and a little while after that, he said to me, "Let's us get married."

"I don't want to get married 'til I'm forty years old and then I am going to go to Alaska," just saying it to get him away. I was about thirty, thirty-one at the time.

Anyway, would you believe it, when I hit forty, he come to me and said, "I'm ready to go to Alaska." It backfired.

At Little Creek I had a lady come in from the nearby Cherokee Indian Reservation to meet with the Home League ladies, our women's group, the ladies of the church. She and her husband were in charge of kids who went to college from Cherokee. I hoped to start a Home League there in Cherokee, but I was transferred before we could get it going. I always wanted to go to India to be a missionary, but the Lord sent me the closest he could…to a different kind of Indian.

Headquarters decides who gets appointed where. A lot of times they ask the corps to see what they think if they want another officer or not, if they are dissatisfied or not. Sometimes they have an officer position open that they want a particular person to get, especially if they fit something that is needed. So I guess that's why I was moved to a mission in the nearest town, to Waynesville.

Major Brown had worked to build the corps there. Waynesville was the largest town in the county and she was doing really good, had an abandoned church building picked out to start the church. Then some folks living nearby were afraid drifters would come around there. It scared them. They hurried up and got some other church to use the place. That disheartened her and she decided to go back to the Mountain Mission.

I was sent to Waynesville, moved there, and lived in town at a house right across from the theater. The Major at that time, Major Gillespie, had told me, "If you don't get busy and do something in Waynesville, they're going to transfer you," so I got busy.

First I had to find a place to meet. I was walking on the street in the edge of town and I looked up at a house with a porch on the side, up high above me on a hill. I saw a bunch of kids and a woman and I says, "Would you care if I had Sunday School here?"

"No, we'd love it," and that's how I started Waynesville. We didn't have a church building, so we'd go to one house for one meeting, go to another house for another meeting, another for another meeting.

Finally this lady says, "You can come here every Sunday morning." She went and got some chairs, put them around in her living room and we had church in there even though the ceilings were too low and we had to go outside to put the flags up.

The folks, bless their hearts, they would open their homes to me, offer a place to have Home League meetings. Women didn't have to belong to the Salvation Army to attend Home League. We opened it up to everybody that wanted to come. They'd have their other churches to go to, too. What tickled me was, the women at the houses I went to wanted to have more attendance than the house the week before and they worked hard to get people to come and it just built up and up.

Home League had a fourfold purpose. We'd have devotions. I used my own materials, anything I could get up. One week a month we'd have a worship service in addition to the devotion. Then the next week we'd have an education program, learn something about the Bible or somebody would come in to talk to us. Another week was for community service where we'd make something for the rest home. The fourth, we'd go to a house, have fellowship, fun, games. What I liked about it, we'd take turns being in charge.

In Waynesville, we also had a Sunday School that was for all ages together and then we would split up by age group. We had what we called the Holiness Meetings, that's the worship service. Then on Sunday night we'd go to another house for a meeting. Finally a lady said, "You know, I've got two houses up on the hill on Frog Level. You can have services up there if you'd like to." We were having Home League in those other houses and growing but it was crowded, and these were empty houses.

I said, "Okay."

I worked hard to help the town people in their life situations, begging them to put money on a house, look for the future. I says, "You don't have to have a big house." One lady in Waynesville, I begged her to buy. I says, "Get a little house. You can build on as you get the money," and she did that. The next Christmas time she was buying stuff for her family and she showed me something in her hand.

She says, "This is for my husband." It was a hat. She was bringing it to the church to put under the tree there for her husband. She had never known what Christmas was except for church, a church Christmas. That was their custom.

I says, "Honey, you need a family Christmas. What you do is, you put the presents under your tree at home. On Christmas morning, you get up and open your gifts."

She came back later and she says, "I never knew something was so wonderful."

There was another woman who got straightened out. Her family had been eating out of garbage cans when I first saw her. Her husband had died. She started coming to church, got right with the Lord, got her life straightened out. She actually got to where when we were having a contest and I said, "I'll give a pie to those who win," she'd stick that arm up, "I'll bring the pies."

We grew so big we finally rented a funeral home in Waynesville. It was great but some people wouldn't come because it was where their parents were laid out, so the corps went down to almost nothing. They transferred me to Georgia in 1968, and the corps in Waynesville moved on down to another building, away from the funeral home, and then the people started coming back.

6

*The sun shall not smite thee by day,*

*nor the moon by night.* **Psalm 121:6**

All those years serving in the Salvation Army I had not been a full officer. At the first, I was just a worker, although I wasn't a volunteer. I did get paid, but I couldn't get retirement benefits. I earned the auxiliary captain level back in 1961, but I needed more.

When I was transferred to Toccoa, Georgia, it was the chance for me to become an officer, take the courses required and then I could become commissioned. Officers go to training college and come out as a lieutenant. Then a captain. Then a major. I joined with the preacher there, Mary Peacock, an auxiliary captain like I was. We took classes in Atlanta, but we had been out in the field for so long, we already knew most of what they told us. Still we had to attend classes. We both got our officership while I was down there. I never was a lieutenant. I went from auxiliary captain to regular captain.

We had to go to Atlanta often, drove back and forth. Atlanta is the main headquarters for the southern territory, West Nyack, New York for the eastern territory, Des Plaines, Iowa for the Central and then we have the western territory out in Long Beach, California. Each territory is divided into divisions and for the Carolinas, that headquarters is in Charlotte, North Carolina.

My commissioning in Atlanta.

The Lord must have had a purpose for me going to Toccoa, more than just taking classes. I don't know for sure unless I was there because the Lord was using me to help Major Peacock. I knew her so well, I knew what she was going to do before she did it. I knew how to work with the major better than anyone else could, although we did have some minor scrapes. She was fussing at me one time about why I was so late getting in. Every night I'd be dog tired because we'd work early in the morning until late in the night. She'd fuss because she had broken her leg and she couldn't get out and go. She was sitting in that chair all day feeling sorry for herself, fussing at me every time I'd come home.

I got so tired of it, I finally said, "Lord, please make her quit talking like this to me or give me gumption to say something." I went to the bathroom, the only place that was private. I used the commode for an altar. That's where I asked the Lord to give me gumption or get her to quit saying that to me.

So the next time I came in, she said it again. "Why come's you're so late? What's wrong?"

"Major," I says, "This lady with me tonight is old. She can't go as fast as she used to. She likes to talk and I get here just as soon as I can." Major looked at me kind of surprised, because I didn't ever say anything back to her.

Next week when I came in, "Did you have a nice trip?"

My Toccoa portrait.
(Troup's Studio)

Sometimes people do that to you, keep on you, and on you. Sometimes you have to speak up. I'm just like a bull in a china closet when things get me worked up. I come out fighting. Not very often, but look out when I do. I've told people, "Listen, you have to ask the Lord first. Be sure that you do because you don't know what will happen if you don't."

When she retired, they wanted me to take over, but I didn't want to. I missed the Smoky Mountains. Toccoa was not my first choice of a place to settle. There is a Tekoa in the Bible and some people thought this was the same word. It was pronounced the same by our accent, but not spelled the same. Tekoa. Toccoa - The name "Toccoa" is from the Cherokee word for beautiful. The only thing the two places had in common, they were both once probably out in the middle of nowhere. 2 Chronicles 20:20, *They rose early in the morning, and went forth into the wilderness of Tekoa: and as they went forth Jehoshaphat stood and said, Hear me, O Judah, and ye inhabitants of Jerusalem: believe in the* LORD *your God, so you shall be established; believe his prophets, so you shall prosper.* It was what we believed about Toccoa, Georgia too. Go to the wilderness, believe in God, so you shall prosper.

I had done a lot of young people's work in the mountains and that's what I did in Toccoa. I had the Girl Guards just like years before when I helped with the Girl Guards when I lived in Pittsburgh. Plus, when Major Peacock wasn't there I had to take over as preacher.

Lots of times children say, "I'm not good enough to be at church." There was a little girl there who didn't think she was good enough for God. She came to me one day when they had started talking about the Lord. She says "Will you ask God and tell him to forgive me?"

It just broke my heart to see children only seven years old coming to me to ask forgiveness for things they didn't do. I said, "Honey, it's not your fault. God forgives everything."

At that time, Brigadier Lord was the one who could change your assignment. He told me, "You know Shelton Laurel doesn't have a leader."

I says, "How about transferring me up there?"

He says, "Okay, get ready."

I says, "Wait long enough, they can't afford for me to get a uniform. Let me get a uniform first." I had to have a new uniform because mine was worn out. Shelton Laurel would pay a good bit on it, but I knew that up there in the mountains they wouldn't have the money to help pay for it.

Girl Guards in Toccoa.

He says, "Hurry up and get your uniform. I'll give you a week."

They had thought maybe if I would get away from the mountains, I would like it better. Not really. It got so hot down there even the police stopped me once and made me roll down my window because it was so hot. You know, my time in Georgia made me think about Joseph in the Old Testament. He was thrown in a pit. He had to go off to live somewhere else but God used him to save his own people from harm. The Lord used him greatly and the Lord used me in Georgia. I didn't know it then, but I must have done a lot more than I thought I did down at Georgia. This woman from there said to me recently, "You know you talked about sanctification so much when you were down there in Georgia. Well, I got sanctified."

I stayed there eight years and then moved. I felt the call back to the mountains.

7

*The Lord shall preserve thee from all evil:*

*He shall preserve thy soul. **Psalm 121:7***

I returned to North Carolina in 1976 and Sib Wilburn joined me in 1978. Sybil Wilburn. Her middle name was Glenn because her daddy wanted a boy, Sybil Glenn. She never wrote it down, would put only Sib. We had met years before in Kentucky, at Mt. Carmel. Sib felt called to preach, wanted to work for the Lord but she had to quit because the money wasn't coming in. She decided to go into teaching and she graduated from Morehead State University when she was fifty-one years old. She still managed to work with the church youth in Kentucky even when she was teaching. She was the type that catches people. Her personality just caught onto them and everybody loved her. She taught thirteen years total, Kentucky three years, then Ohio.

My friend and my
helper, Sib Wilburn.

I begged her to come to North Carolina to help me. I knew she missed those years she was working for the Lord and I says, "When you come down here you won't have to worry. I'll just call you my little puppy." I'm short, but she was shorter, just like a little doll. In some ways she was a lot better than I was. She had more education than I did. When I asked her to come to help me, she said, "I can't do it until I know that's what the Lord wants."

In the end it was the story of the wells that helped her make a decision to move. In the Bible, book of Joshua and again in Judges, there was a man, Caleb. Moses promised him land because he and one other spy were the only two who thought that with God's help they could conquer the Promised Land. He was right and the people of Israel entered the Promised Land when he was an old man, but he got his land. When his daughter got married he gave part of it for her dowry, but it was dry desert. She needed water and she asked him for the springs, too. He was a loving father, gave her not only the upper springs but the lower springs as well.

Sib had just finished reading that Bible story about the wells and the abundance of water when I called her on the phone. Before she spoke I said, "Oh, Sib, guess what? I have enough water here to house twelve families."

She was so shocked. She says, "That's my answer." She came down here then, joined me at Shelton Laurel, and oh, they loved her.

Soon after she arrived, Sib and I planned a trip to Germany. Because I was in uniform in my picture, they said, "We can't accept this." So I had to go get another picture made. We knew some officers in Germany to stay with and drive us around, ended up in seven countries, but we weren't allowed to go through the Iron Curtain. When we were in London, I went to the Salvation Army headquarters, and then over to a museum and the trading post and to see where General William Booth and his wife were buried.

Back at Shelton Laurel, I was the preacher and Sib was helping me. On Sundays we had Sunday School in the morning and then Holiness Meeting, a youth meeting in the afternoon, then Salvation Meeting that same night. We also had Home League meetings during the week, but they were more casual. For example, at one of our programs, one member went out into the woods, cut a tree down, stripped the bark off and showed us how to cane a chair bottom.

Being a woman preaching in the mountains wasn't easy. Paul in his letter to Galatians said, "*Neither female nor male…for you are one in Christ.*" The men didn't always explain things, though. They were the only ones that got an education and the women didn't understand.

They'd say, "What's he talking about?" It was disturbing the audience. That's why Paul wanted them to keep quiet.

The Bible verses I would use for my sermon would just come to me. When you get in your mind what you want, then you go to the scriptures.

Can't find it? You look it up in the commentary and find it there or at least something about it. Most of the time, it just came to me what to say. I talked to the people just like I'm talking now, just preach them the Word, tell them what the Lord said.

Meeting at Little Creek.
(©RayRouserPhotography)

In 1983 I moved down to the mission field in Hot Springs, stationed at Little Creek, Bonnie Hill and Sleepy Valley. I lived in Hot Springs and for Sunday morning meetings I would drive first to Bonnie Hill for the Holiness Meeting and Sunday School, then down to Sleepy Valley, about eight miles away for another Holiness Meeting. After lunch I would drive over to Little Creek and have the third Holiness Meeting and then go back to Sleepy Valley and have a youth meeting and finally a Salvation meeting that night, all in one day. It would vary how many people attended, average about twenty-five. The Salvation meetings were for telling the gospel to those who didn't know the Lord. Holiness Meetings had depth to them and developed the plan of salvation more.

When I was assigned to Little Creek before, the women sat on one side of the room, the men on the other, an old custom. When I returned from Georgia and went back, they weren't sitting on separate sides any more. Times had changed a bit.

I was a regular preacher by then, but Sib helped me with the youth work. We did everything and I was busy since we didn't have anybody to help us do anything. All those meetings on Sunday and then I had Wednesday night prayer meeting, then had to collect three days a week. I'd go out and get an offering and for a shy person like me, that was hard. I would go to business places and collect and turn the donations in to the office headquarters. That money would be used to help people in the community.

A session with one of my many youth groups.

Major Brown had taught me to take a tambourine to do the collecting. The tambourine in the Salvation Army was for more than music. We'd used it for collecting donations, turn it over, hold it out, expecting the people to put money in it. Major Brown said to go in the places and ask them. Ugh. It was awful, some of the places I went to. I complained to her once that it was hard for me to do. She put her arm around me and said, "Yes, but it makes you humble."

It was just me and my tambourine. Every time I would get to the door, at each and every door, I'd have to pray, "Lord give me grace to go in. Give me grace to go in," because I couldn't stand it. A fellow took a beer can one time and put it in my tambourine. I don't know what kind of look I gave him. I guess I looked pitiful. "Oh, I'm sorry," and he took it out.

Most people were nice. If they couldn't give or didn't want to give they'd say "I can't give today." I think it's according to the way you approached them.

I also rang the bells for the kettles. The Salvation Army collects money for missions at Christmas using kettles outside stores and on streets. Cold. I do mean cold work that went on even through rain and snow, didn't matter what the weather. I did enjoy watching the mothers with their children. They would give them coins to drop in, instruct them about what they were doing, why they were giving.

I never did like to collect. In fact, that's the only way the officer got me to go to Winston-Salem in 1986, because I sure didn't want to leave the mountains.

"You won't have to collect if you go."

"Okay, I'll go."

Well, I didn't have to collect with the tambourine any more, I didn't have to ring the bells any more, but from then on, I did go around at Christmas and collect the kettles at the end of the day.

In the Salvation Army, you don't usually take somebody with you when you transfer. I said to Colonel Holt, the man in charge, "You're moving me over to Winston-Salem. Can I bring Sib with me?"

With Sib.

"By all means, bring her." I was shocked. I thought I was going to have to fight to bring her, but you know, she wouldn't have had any other place to go. Sib was up close to seventy years old by then, but she was still active and could help. I guess he had told the people there, "Major Frese finally decided to come and she's bringing this old lady with her, too."

It was a good decision because everybody in Winston-Salem loved her. After she got there and he got to knowing her, it was fine. She just won his heart. People were like that about her, just loved her. She went as a volunteer, did the cooking, helping with the activities. Some of the people in Winston got to fussing about wanting her to come out and do this and do that. I just got so tired of it one day, I says, "Listen, you folks just keep on demanding things from her but she doesn't get one cent for cooking for you guys."

"Huh?"

"She does all this voluntarily."

One lady came up to me three times and said, "She don't get anything?"

"Not a cent."

The people there were good, real nice. Only thing was, they had been a little rough on Sib, but once I changed that, they were good to her and pitched in to help in that kitchen.

We were assigned to Winston-Salem to work with senior citizens. That was our purpose, run the activities for seniors. We worked there every day and fed them a meal, usually cooked by Sib. Then we had a devotional. I even had one of the retired officers, Major Dot Rickard do a Bible study. She's another one the Lord sent to help me, mentor me. It was a job just to keep up with the activities. I'd work up late at night. The people there would go to their own churches on Sundays and I went to my own church since I didn't have a corps assignment, just the center and then Sunday School at Southside.

Dot and Sib hard at work.

We had a large black community there. Some fellows were making fun of this one boy because he was going to Sunday School and I was a white preacher and they were black. They got him riled up. The door on the corps was painted white and we had just scrubbed it, cleaned it up. He went and throwed rotten tomatoes at the door. I took him in my office, talked to him kindly, "What did we do to you? Did I do something to hurt you to make you throw those tomatoes on that door?" He didn't have a word to say. He left. Next thing I know, he was scrubbing this door down, cleaning it off.

Another time these fellows were playing with a kite, the men were. They got one caught up in a tree and came over to me, asked me if I could lend them a ladder to get the kite. I said, "Yeah, I saw you over there playing with the kite. Yes, go get the ladder."

"You're different. You don't act like everybody else. You're so kind."

People were coming in from the main part of town, they liked it so well. Some of the black folks in other places begged our black clients to come to their place instead. "No, we like it here. We don't want to go down there." There were white folks as well, about half and half.

One of the social workers was after a lady in our group because her house was a historical house and her son wanted to put it in the historical registry in Winston-Salem. They would have to move the house and put it down with the rest of the houses where the historical site was. They were going to get her a trailer in place of it, but they wanted to know if she was able physically and mentally to handle it. I says, "Why, yes, she's been preaching and everything else. Why wouldn't she manage her own place?"

When that social worker walked in, she saw the people. "I can't believe that you've got this here on this side of town. You've got as many white people as you do black."

Winston-Salem is where I learned ceramics, where I first started and I've been doing them ever since. They already had a ceramics program before I got there, so I told them the same thing I told them in the mountains years before when I first arrived, "You've got to help me."

I went in and made the announcement, "I don't know anything about ceramics, never have done it in my life. You've got to teach me." They pitched in and helped. It thrilled them to death to be able to help teach me.

People started flocking in. They didn't have to pay a fee for the class. They just bought the stock. The Army paid for the meals we served, but the people paid for their own forms for their ceramics. We could get it cheaper and I would go get the raw stuff so they wouldn't have to pay so much for it.

The first thing I ever made, have it sitting as you come in the door of my house now, a chicken. Now I could paint that chicken, but I had an artist that was in the class do the eyes and details. Ooh, she was a good artist. The shape of these ceramics was already formed, poured. We'd clean it. Then we'd take it to the back room and fire it. Then paint it and then fire it again. If we put decals on it, we'd fire it again. We had our own kiln there in the back. It was electric, but you had to light it, just a little stick that they put in even though it was electric.

They had taught me how to load the kiln and put the stick in there to burn it, but I wasn't sure if I was doing it right, didn't know for sure how to light it. I went out in the main room to where Major Dot Rickard was playing the piano. The rest of the people were around her and I just made another big announcement. "I got this still ready, but I don't know how to fire it."

Everybody got real quiet. Nobody said a word.

"What'd you say?"

I says, "I can't light this still."

Major Dot said, "Do you know what you said?" and I looked at her sort of funny. She said, "I don't know anything about lighting a still, but I can light this kiln for you!" Oh, they had a big time over that and they never let me live it down.

I carried over something else from the mountains, a skill Major Brown taught me years before, backing in to park my car. When I was in Winston-Salem they made fun of me for backing in, but before I left, every car was parked backed in.

I don't know why God sent me there away from the mountains, but I figure He had a place for me. My mission was different in Winston than the mountains. Home League I loved more than anything else and when I was in Winston-Salem, I had one. I'd take them on trips, do everything with them. At my Home League meeting in 1989 we had people bring their special dolls and we made a display of them. I gave each of them a ceramic shell as a favor, fixed it so it would be an African violet face. I also had a youth group and a Bible study just for kids. They kept pushing me to come do some stuff over at the corps. I said, "Listen, you do your job and let me do my job."

Another meeting.

Coming to Winston-Salem just blessed Sib's heart. They loved her there. Sib made it nice because she told me after, "You know, I'm so glad I went to Winston-Salem. I've always felt bad because I couldn't finish working as a missionary in Kentucky. In Winston, I felt like my ministry was fulfilled, like I was honoring God." See when she quit ministry to go to college to get her degree to teach, she felt like she left the Lord even though the Lord had called her to work in the field. She said, "Made me feel good. It filled my calling."

My retirement service was held in Winston-Salem on June 30, 1991. They said I had "done a superior job in all assignments, preferring to work behind-the-scenes, in a quiet and effective manner." Lot of folks want publicity, but I cared less about it, didn't realize they were going to write that in my pamphlet. They wrote about me doing things for them, but I had done them quietly, didn't broadcast what I was doing.

I did what I wanted to do.

No.

I did what the Lord wanted me to do.

8

*The LORD shall preserve thy going out and thy coming in*

*from this time forth, and even for evermore.* **Psalm 121:8**

I had been preparing for my retirement for ten years before I actually retired. I knew I could get retirement benefits because I was an officer, but I needed a place to live. I owned some land near Bonnie Hill, beside a creek where they baptized people, but I decided

Returning with Sib at my side.

to build closer to Shelton Laurel where there were more people around. Sib and I started building the house where I live now in 1981, during the mission years, through the time we lived in Winston-Salem. The house was ready when I retired so I returned to Shelton Laurel for the third time. I went back to the name Lorraine because that is what I am on my social security, although people still call me Jean.

I left everything behind in Pennsylvania when I first moved to the Smoky Mountains and it turned out to be a good decision. I look back now, who's in Pittsburgh? None of the family is there any more. Nowadays they don't make hats and that's what I was training for back then. Hats went out of style. I would have been without a job, even though one of the ladies begged me to go to her shop, I would have had to learn something else. The Evangeline Residence where I stayed, it's gone. I had no reason to return to Pennsylvania.

When I retired in 1991, everything about the house was paid for and completed like I wanted. I remember when I was a child at home we used to have just one heater in the floor. I said, "I don't want that." You'd freeze to death when you went to bed. I made sure this house was warm. I didn't build a fancy house. I wanted a convenient house, but one with air conditioning.

Home Sweet Home.

They all made fun of me because mountain people had no air conditioning, but then afterwards, a whole lot of them got it. The fellow was hunting the house to work on the air conditioning, hunting and hunting for it, couldn't find the house. He went down to a neighbor. "There's nobody that has air conditioning but that millionaire up on top of the hill." They thought only millionaires had air, but Shelton Laurel's hot even if it is in the mountains. When I was up at Maple Springs, it was higher in elevation and a lot colder than here.

I have a sign as you come in the door, "The Doll House." Maybe it looks like a doll house, but it's made for me, cabinets short, so I can reach everything. I knew it was going to be a small house, so I made as few partitions as I could to make it look bigger inside. People come in and they're shocked to see it's bigger than it looks from the outside. I've got too much stuff crammed in it now. One person told me the house was a Cracker Barrel. One said it was a museum. My problem, it's hard for me to get rid of stuff, they mean so much, and so it keeps collecting.

The kitchen cabinets are all wormy chestnut. I would find boards for building them in different places, even found some down in Georgia. The kitchen table is actually a bed, turned the headpiece flat and then somebody made some legs for it. The beds were Army beds, made out of wormy chestnut. Some furniture came from the big house in Winston-Salem since they didn't need it any more. Sib chose the pie safe and I took the bookcase where I store the Salvation Army dinnerware that I got when I was in England. When I had Salvation Army guests, I used Salvation Army dishes.

I was driving through Michigan and I saw an old chandelier out in a person's yard, throwing it away. I knocked on the door and asked if I could have it. They said yes and I took it. I brought it to the electric shop and, "You're going to put that in a new house?"

I said, "Yeah."

He said, "Awwh." I put glass globes around it to protect the light bulbs. I thought about getting little shades, but I like it plain like that, gives off more light.

There is also an old wall lamp in the living room, an oil lamp converted to electric. I gave Captain another one like it for the archives because they both came from Little Creek Corps back when they changed to electric lights. The oil lamp on the piano was Sib's, brought down from Ohio, and the couch, too.

There's a carport to the side and I still back the car into it like Major Brown taught me. I've always named my cars starting with my first, Black Beauty. Next I had Blue Bird. My third one was painted white and since we weren't really allowed to have a white car back then, I named it Forbidden. Then I had Blue Jay, a former bootleg car. It had a taillight that worked separate from the other lights so it could be used as a signal to say the liquor was ready. Somewhere along the line I had the Red Cardinal. I had a white station wagon,

White Dove, that I had to buy so I could carry Sib's wheelchair. The car I have now I named "Angel Car" because I have tiny angel statues all through it. There's a decal, too, an angel hat with "hattitude" written on it, and a quote by Ralph Waldo Emerson, "Let us be silent that we may hear the whispers of God."

For the first few years, I had a porch on the back of my house. I was sitting out there eating one day and I had a red hat on. A hummingbird came by and I had to duck. I eventually closed the porch in and made a third bedroom because I got tired of sleeping on the couch in the living room whenever we had company.

The one thing people notice most about my house is the railing that runs across the living room dividing it from the kitchen. At first I didn't have it and the room was open, but the dogs could get up on the couch, knock over the ceramics. So I got full sized sheets of plywood that I would slide across to keep the dogs out. I got tired of doing that, so Major Barton, Timothy Barton, designed and built a railing just the right size. He painted it dark to match the cherry board that is on the shelf next to it. I hang quilts over the rail sometimes to add color. It's like an indoor fence, just a little shorter than my waist, has a gate in the middle. Looks more like a church altar rail, but it's not. It's a dog fence.

Dogs weren't always a part of my life, but they turned out to be important to me. Major Brown gave me one of the kittens from an old mother cat that had taken up at Maple Springs. That started my love of pets. I sort of took them in because they came to me. When I went to Toccoa, Major Peacock gave me her two dogs, Dachshunds, that she couldn't take care of any more. That's what got me interested in that particular breed. Then when they died, I got Gretel. She was born around the year 2000. I was hunting for a red Dachshund, couldn't find one anywhere around here. We found one in a town about an hour away, Rutherfordton. Sib picked up this one little dog, set it in her lap and said, "It looks like Rufus."

"I'll take it."

Back before I retired, I had gotten Rufus, Rufus Jasper. He was a dog I took care of for a neighbor who was too sick to handle him anymore. I said, "Let me have him. I'll pay you for it." I paid him three dollars, got the dog, brought it up here. I let him run loose so he could go down and visit the man any time he wanted. I asked him later, "Did he ever come visit you?"

"He comes one time in the morning, every day." He finally had to go into a rest home, so I took the dog there for them to visit.

Then we had Sunny Sam. A preacher from the Methodist Church was keeping the dog, and she had to go back to school. She brought the dog to us and we'd take care of it while she was gone.

A fellow once came to the door. He said, "I'm counting the census. How many do you have living here?"

"Well, I got, let's see, Rufus Jasper," so I counted out loud, Rufus and then Sam and I named Wilburn. I didn't say Sib, I used her last name. That sounded like three men, but I wasn't telling a lie.

"Well, you'll get something in the mail after while about it," and he took off. That night, when I turned the news on, his picture flashed up. They must have caught him right after he left my house because he had the same shirt on. They were arresting him for going around stealing from people. Seems like the Lord just took care of me. Again.

We also had a black dog called Shadow. He was down at the dumpster with a pack of dogs. We'd feed them and we knew they needed help. We called the Humane Society to come and get all the dogs, the whole bunch of them, but this one hid. Finally, Sib said, "Would you get him?" We went to the dumpster and here come this dog out, right to me.

Gretel was a different story. She was the first puppy I ever had. It's like having a youngin. I said, "Sib, will you take care of her until she gets a little bit older. I'll take care of your dog."

Gretel

Her dog Cheenie, a Pomeranian, was just a little older, both of them born the same year. Cheenie Rose. We liked the name Cheenie, but we had to have two names to register her, so we gave her the name Rose.

Gretel lived about twelve years, just died recently. I prayed, "God, don't let me go before the dogs die because I don't want them to go without me. They wouldn't want to live with another person."

Cheenie's on her last leg now, I have to give her heart pills, medicine,

Cheenie

just like me. We're getting old together.

I still stay active, but there are things that slow me down. Even now, God provides. Not too long ago, I couldn't find my hearing aid, looked everywhere for it. I said, "Lord, please show me where that thing is." It cost almost three thousand dollars. I was thinking that in the Bible times the Lord spoke to people, yet it seems like He doesn't speak like that today. But this came to my mind, just like the Lord was speaking to me, "Go to bed, I'll show you in the morning."

I'd still hunt and I'd pray, "Lord, please help me find it."

"Go to bed, you'll find it in the morning." So I did. When morning came, I got ready to walk the dog, put on my coat, reached in my pocket and there it was. It was in my coat pocket that I take the dog out with. I can't believe it, but it was proof, too. The Lord still talks even if it's through subconscious.

They told us when we retire we should have a hobby. I guess if you would say I have a hobby, it would be ceramics. We take turns leading the Wednesday meeting up here at Shelton Laurel, so I started helping with ceramics. "Do you care if we have ceramics?"

"Oh, we'd love it."

I figured any time it's my turn to lead, that's what we would do. It can be for men and women, the adults. I try to find things that are not too hard to do. This last time we did a lamb, just finished this year in time for Easter. Since there are husband and wives, I do different figures, the lamb standing up for the man, sitting down for the woman. I purchase the ceramics in Newport, Tennessee because it's closer to here than Asheville, plus I get gas cheaper in the other state, fill up every time I go. The lambs are not hard to do, just paint the white body and then black ears and feet, do the face. The people are able to clean it themselves instead of me taking it to Newport between firings because one of my friends, Dr. Karen Hartman gave me enough money to buy the right tools. We have it fired at the kilns in Newport, bring it here to put the glaze on it, then there to fire it again. Actually, it takes three different weeks to do a project. I made a friend of mine, Dr. Edith Halpkee, lambs like those. She raises sheep but these ceramic ones weren't like hers. Hers have black legs, so I made her a new set that looked more like her own lambs.

I work on ceramic Christmas trees all year round, try to do one a week to be ready to give away for Christmas. My doctors, I gave them a tree. Kidney clinic, I gave everyone of them a tree. I just enjoy doing it. At Christmas time where there are patients whose families don't go to visit them in the rest home much, I take them trees.

When I first moved in here I decorated the house special for Christmas and brought out my ceramic figures. I'd put cotton on tables to look like snow. I had it fixed up fancy, did ceramic deer and a sleigh, put it by the coffee table, had a little village. I finally stopped putting things away. I keep some things out all year round, including about five ceramic Christmas trees that I keep lit.

Smiling faces with Major Dot
Rickard at the 2002 SAROA

I stay busy, still doing the Lord's work, doing all kinds of activities besides ceramics. For a while I liked to go to officers' councils at Myrtle Beach and the SAROA, Salvation Army Retired Officers Association. I attend Home League meetings, although now they've changed its title to Women's Ministries. I go when the conferences are up here, especially in Gatlinburg. That way I can drive back and forth because I like to stay with my baby. Dogs are a nuisance, but they're company.

There's an annual event, the Southern Bible Conference I attend every year at Lake Junaluska, about twenty miles away. People come from everywhere to that, from up north, from everywhere. In 1998 General Eva Burrows came to Shelton Laurel from headquarters in London on her way to Lake Junaluska. She came here because she was the speaker at the conference and had heard so much about the Mountain Mission. A lot of other important people have come to hear our music, love to come to the Mountain Singing while they were at the Bible Conference. Lot of times, we'd have the speaker come out here, say a few words. We would schedule a singing just before the conference, with singing on Sunday, then the conference began on Sunday night.

Cooling in the shade at the Singing on the Mountain.

We called it a Singing Convention. We originally used the old shape-note style of singing. That's a lost art of singing that people don't do much any more. Even our conventions now don't use that style, have gone for more gospel type singing.

What they used to do, each corps in the mountain mission would have their songsters come sing. Then we'd have a guest group. Major Brown had thousands of visitors come to Maple Springs to the

convention when it was up at the top of the mountain where their cemetery is now. We also had conventions at Poplar Gap. In 2002 the Singing on the Mountain was dedicated to me. "Major Jean Frese, for her love and service to the mountains," the program said. The picture on the cover of the program was me. The horse picture was actually drawn by Bonita Swanger from two separate photographs, my head from one and the horse from another.

You don't always get a chance to know what you did in your life and this honor sort of let me know. For the most part, you just have to do things by faith, but it makes you feel so good to find out that you did hit some people right. It's encouragement to you. I've had children that would come up on the mountain, live with us two years or so, and years later, like at this convention, they would tell me the only happiness they ever had as a child was those years. There's different organizations that help people having a hard time, but people that's working and have a struggle, that's the ones I've always tried to help. When I would see people with talent, I

A Shelton Laurel honor.

became their motivation. Mountain people are smart. They just didn't always have the opportunity to develop.

Music is still a part of the Salvation Army, always has been. At Shelton Laurel now the young people play timbrels so beautifully. A timbrel is a musical instrument like a tambourine, but the timbrel has a double ring of cymbals around it. The single ring ones are called tambourines. They do a beautiful job shaking them and they don't even sing along. They might play a tape with a music background to go along with it, but they can so well do without any accompaniment.

Captain Susan Graf is their leader. She's musical too, can play a horn. She lives in the quarters over here and she's another person the Lord has sent into my life. She checks on me and if I'm not doing what I'm regularly supposed to do, she either calls or comes over and sees what's the trouble. She's wonderful, so good with the young people, knows how to work with children who have problems, too. The members at Shelton Laurel are concerned about me and call to find out how I am doing, if there is anything I need, if I have any problems at all, "Call me if you need help. I'll take you to the doctor. I'll do this or that." I'm thankful they want to do that. It makes you feel good, not necessarily to get the attention, just the idea that this care comes from their hearts. One day after surgery, they came in and

July 2012 Singing on the Mountain at Shelton Laurel. Captain Graf on far right.

scrubbed my floors, did what they could to help me. It means a lot to me, just the idea they are there for me.

When you work for the Lord, you will have troubles, because Satan doesn't like it. Through the years many people came to my rescue, helped me in all kinds of ways. That's what the Lord's done for me, sent the right person. Every time I get in a tight spot, there's someone right there to get me out of it and encourage me.

The Lord always provided me with somebody, even up to now with Captain Susan Graf and Shelton Laurel. Dr. Karen Hartman is the latest, takes me out to dinner every two weeks, makes me feel good there's somebody compassionate around that cares about me. That's how I was drawn to her because I would watch her with people. She has a wonderful compassion.

With Dr. Karen Hartman.

Of all the churches I worked in this area, Shelton Laurel and Sleepy Valley are the only two that are left, but our influence can still be felt. Many churches in the valley have trained leaders from the Salvation Army because we taught leadership. But see, people couldn't get jobs up here and a lot of them moved away. There just weren't that many people left to support a corps. Oh, we hated that Maple Springs was gone. When it was sold, first someone bought it for a drug, alcohol rehab center and it's been through several owners since then. They'd take people up there to get them straightened out. They had services, but they had it in a circle because of the rehab sessions. They had to straighten the floor because it was originally slanted so everybody in the back could see the speaker.

There was a fellow that used to be in my Sunday school class when I was on horseback. When Brigadier Henry came, he got converted. Then one day he looked in the window at Maple Springs when it was rehab and he cried. He said, "This is where I got saved and they are drinking on the pulpit." The men from the rehab that hadn't gotten straightened out had slipped liquor and they were sitting on the altar drinking.

The current officer in Hot Springs is really tremendous. The corps was just almost nothing down there. He's got it built up until now it's a beautiful place. He's got two thrift shops. Sometimes people don't have a missionary atmosphere, zeal. He does. He understands the mission, like Sib did with her missionary zeal.

Sib and I were both active after I retired. In fact, Brigadier Henry was in charge of Little Creek and he would often be away, preaching. He begged us to go over there and take over while he was gone. We replaced him one time for a whole year.

We would attend meetings and one time Brigadier Henry was preaching in his house at a cottage prayer meeting. Just right out in the middle of the message, we shouted, "Brigadier, move!"

He didn't.

"Brigadier, move!"

"What do you want me to move for?"

"Brigadier, move!!" We were so persistent, all of us, so he moved.

"Now look up over your head." There was a big snake ready to drop right on him. I had read the stories in the Bible representing the snake as the devil and that's what it looked like then, Satan slithering around to interrupt us. That snake was a reminder that Satan is always watching and waiting for his chance. After you work with the Lord a long time, seems like Satan works harder to stop you. No matter how much you love the Lord, old Satan is right there.

I've found a couple of snakes in my house over the years. I looked on the shower curtain once and there was a snake right over my head ready to drop. I put a ladder outside, up to the windowsill near the tub. It did not go out down that ladder until dark. I said,

"The Lord took care of those snakes for me and the Lord took care of me. Old Satan, he's on the run because I don't want him."

When I first retired, Sib and I divided up the living expenses. That's what was rough on me when Sib died in 2007 and I had to pay all the bills where before we had split the expenses. It wasn't a whole lot, but it was enough to get by better. It was safety, too, protection.

I told Sib when we moved back to Shelton Laurel I would take care of her and she wouldn't have to go to a rest home. When she had that aneurysm, she got a wheelchair, and even though she could walk, she wouldn't do much of it. She was ready to go home to the Lord, but she lived two years afterwards. When we die we say that we are promoted to glory, how Sib believed, that she was ready to be promoted. I had decided to be buried at the Salvation Army Cemetery at headquarters in Atlanta because there weren't any of my relatives living near enough here to take care of the grave. I made arrangements to be buried there and I said to Sib, "Why don't we just bury you down there, too?"

Just before she died, she said, "Are you going to do what you planned?"

I said, "Yeah," and didn't think anything about it. After Sib's death, we went to Atlanta and had services down there at the graveyard. As that box dropped down, those words came to me, "Are you going to be buried like you planned?" It just said to me I did wrong. It was wrong for me to bury her there. Then on the way home, I got to thinking, planning to go pick her back up. I was going to get some fellows to come with me and we'd dig her up, bring her home, shouldn't be too hard since she had been cremated and the box was small.

I asked some of the people at church, "Do you think it's wrong for me to go down there and get Sib and bring her back up here?"

"I don't know why you took her down there in the beginning."

I went to talk to my friend, Dr. Hartman. "Do you think it's strange that I want to do that?"

She says, "Well, no. I'll take you and we'll spend the night with my mama and go the next day and pick her up and bring her home." So I called and they had her ready for me, had cleaned up the box to bring her up here. We had another service for her, took her out and buried her here in the cemetery right beside her sister, the one from Ohio. Sib loved that song about the dove, "On the Wings of a Snow

White Dove," so she had put that on her sister's tombstone. On hers I put, "My Jesus I Love Thee."

"What can I put on mine?" I went through several options, nothing fit. Then I thought I'd just put, "Thank you Lord for giving me the call to the mountains." I put it on the tombstone and it's already there in the cemetery on the hill, under a tree, within sight of my home.

Looking back at all I've accomplished, I know I didn't do it alone, but with the Lord's help, like King David wrote in Psalm 121, *My help cometh from the Lord.* My prayer of praise that I say again and again is simple. "Thank you Lord for bringing me to the mountains."

*Psalm 121*
*David*

*I will lift up mine eyes unto the hills,*
*from whence cometh my help.*
*My help cometh from the* LORD,
*which made heaven and earth.*
*He will not suffer thy foot to be moved:*
*he that keepeth thee will not slumber.*
*Behold, he that keepeth Israel*
*shall neither slumber nor sleep.*
*The* LORD *is thy keeper:*
*the* LORD *is thy shade upon thy right hand.*
*The sun shall not smite thee by day,*
*nor the moon by night.*
*The* LORD *shall preserve thee from all evil:*
*he shall preserve thy soul.*
*The* LORD *shall preserve thy going out*
*and thy coming in from this time forth,*
*and even for evermore.*
*Amen*

86

# ABOUT THE AUTHOR

Author Gretchen Griffith spent many pleasant hours in a labor of love collecting the life story of her mother's cousin, Lorraine Frese, also known as Major Jean. Like her cousin, Gretchen was born in Pennsylvania and eventually moved to western North Carolina, where, also like her cousin, she taught school. The comparison ends there with a unique glimpse into the world of this devoted mountain missionary. Gretchen remembers listening to these tales as a child at family gatherings and now has compiled them in *Called to the Mountain* as an honor to her family.

Visit Gretchen at www.gretchengriffith.com.

Made in the USA
San Bernardino, CA
21 May 2014